Missing the boat

The failure to internationalize
American higher education

CRAUFURD D. GOODWIN

Duke University

and

MICHAEL NACHT

University of Maryland

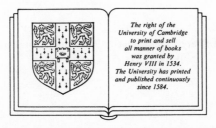

The right of the
University of Cambridge
to print and sell
all manner of books
was granted by
Henry VIII in 1534.
The University has printed
and published continuously
since 1584.

CAMBRIDGE UNIVERSITY PRESS
Cambridge
New York   Port Chester   Melbourne   Sydney

Published by the Press Syndicate of the University of Cambridge
The Pitt Building, Trumpington Street, Cambridge CB2 1RP
40 West 20th Street, New York, NY 10011, USA
10 Stamford Road, Oakleigh, Melbourne 3166, Australia

© Cambridge University Press 1991

First published 1991

Printed in the United States of America

Library of Congress Cataloging-in-Publication Data
Goodwin, Craufurd D. W.
Missing the boat : the failure to internationalize American higher
education /Craufurd D. Goodwin and Michael Nacht.
          p.   cm.
          Includes index.
          ISBN 0-521-40213-1 (hardcover)
1. Foreign study.   2. Educational exchanges.   3. Educational exchanges –
United States – Case studies.   I. Nacht, Michael.   II. Title.
          LB2375.G66   1991
370.19′6–dc20   90-49059
                                                                          CIP

British Library Cataloguing-in-Publication Data applied for
ISBN 0 521 40213 1 hardback

other principal objectives espoused by the U.S. institutions. For example, it was not unusual, they found, for a college to identify the Pacific Rim as a high-priority area yet continue to maintain study-abroad programs solely in Western Europe.

In addition to these studies, which have prompted much discussion, the publications and research have led to a series of meetings at the National Association for Foreign Students Affairs, the American Council on Education, the Council of Graduate Schools, and other professional societies. It is our hope that this report will continue the tradition of highlighting the importance of the topic and will assist CIES in generating discussion and proposing solutions to the problems documented.

Before the authors began their travels, we had several long discussions that provided me with an opportunity to share dozens of "impressions" of faculty success stories and an equal number about failures or frustrations. Goodwin and Nacht had many of these observations confirmed in the course of their campus visits. Their experience on the campus of Colorado State University (CSU) at Fort Collins was an especially poignant example of this complex subject. Walking down the center mall of the CSU campus, they could not help noticing that a yellow ribbon was tied around each of the massive tree trunks lining the path. These ribbons were a graphic symbol of the deeply felt pain on the campus caused by the plight of Thomas Sutherland, a professor of animal science in the College of Agriculture who, while a visiting faculty member at the American University in Beirut, was kidnapped in 1985. Professor Sutherland's experience – that of an accomplished agricultural specialist who went abroad to teach and provide technical assistance, only to get caught up in the vicissitudes of Middle East politics – dramatizes the complex subject addressed in this book. Fortunately, the Sutherland tragedy is an exception, rather than the rule. Nonetheless, the profile of faculty observations on their international experience reveals areas that badly need thoughtful consideration from policy makers in our colleges and universities.

We are most appreciative of The Pew Charitable Trusts' support, which made this study possible. I wish to acknowledge

There was not universal acceptance or agreement with all the findings in their report, but the discussions that followed served to help shape lively debate of the issues on individual campuses and within a large national constituency of international education advocates.

This study was followed by two additional projects for IIE that focused specifically on students from developing countries who had studied in the United States. In 1983 they interviewed returned Brazilian students in three major cities, São Paulo, Rio de Janeiro, and Brasilia. The findings of that study, reported in *Fondness and Frustration,* revealed that although the Brazilians were highly positive about their experience in the United States, they returned home frustrated either because they could not always apply the skills they had learned or because their skills declined over time as a result of insufficient resources and stimulation in the home environment.

To pursue this subject further, they undertook a major comparative study in 1984–5 on the problem of intellectual and professional decay, using three countries, Mexico, Indonesia, and Turkey. Again, they interviewed hundreds of individuals in these three countries who worked in universities, government agencies, and the private sector, all of whom had studied in the United States, mostly at the graduate level. In that report, *Decline and Renewal* (IIE, 1986), they described in detail the programs and techniques that have been developed to maintain the skills and knowledge base of third-world professionals who had studied in the United States. They noted that one shortcoming of the current practices was the lack of consistent alumni contact (except for fundraising purposes) between U.S. academic institutions and their foreign student alumni.

Lastly, in 1987 Goodwin and Nacht examined the phenomenon at colleges and universities of studying abroad. Again, following their methodology, they conducted interviews at diverse institutions in California, Texas, Illinois, and Massachusetts. They examined in considerable detail the incentives and disincentives for American students to spend time overseas. The study highlighted the relative lack of consistency between these programs and the

raise whatever issues were relevant to the subject of faculty experiences abroad. They also shared ideas and perspectives they had
heard expressed in places they had visited previously. They purposely sought out skeptics as well as ardent supporters. Upon
return they digested the hundreds of pages of notes and organized
a report in useful analytical categories. Their study of the faculty
issues, which takes the form of their previous reports, is a provocative analytical essay that we believe is timely and relevant
to the policy-making community.

To put this report in a larger context, a brief description of the
authors' four previous studies on aspects of international education is in order. Their first report, *Absence of Decision* (1983),
commissioned by the Institute of International Education (IIE),
explored the policy issues associated with foreign students in
American colleges and universities. The study included visits to
a large number of institutions primarily in Florida, Ohio, and California. In this study they began the pattern of wide-ranging interviews rather than statistical surveys to explore the topic.

Among the principal findings of the first study were the following:

(a) Most colleges and universities place the subject of for-
    eign students low on their list of priorities, and knowl-
    edge and interest in the issue become significant only
    when the percentage of foreign students within particu-
    lar departments or schools exceeds 15 or 20 percent of
    the student body.
(b) Most institutions have not thought through in much de-
    tail the economic, educational, political, and organiza-
    tional issues associated with the presence of large num-
    bers of foreign students on their campuses.
(c) The "humanist presumption" that the foreign student is
    an enriching and social presence on the U.S. campus
    needs to be supported with stronger evidence.
(d) The marginal cost of the foreign student body has rarely
    been computed, although there have been any number
    of claims as to what these costs might be.

ence among the faculty on the internationalization of U.S. campuses in general? What are the central issues for debate that command further attention?

Goodwin and Nacht approached this report as they had their earlier reports by a system of extensive campus visits and interviews. They went to thirty-seven institutions of higher education in four different regions: ten in the Pacific northwestern states of Washington and Oregon, seven in the southeastern states of Georgia and South Carolina, ten in Massachusetts, and ten in the Rocky Mountain states of Utah and Colorado. Most of the institutions had not been visited by Goodwin and Nacht in the course of their previous studies. (A full list of the institutions visited is contained in the Appendix.) The institutions were selected intentionally for their heterogeneity; they are public and private, urban and rural, large and small, secular and church related. We specifically chose institutions that had a reputation for substantial interest and experience in international programs and those about which we knew very little. Our desire was to seek a cross-section of all types of institutions and not to focus solely on those that are especially active internationally.

Given the financial and time constraints of this study, they spent a day or half a day at each institution. They held discussions with faculty from a broad range of disciplines and with senior administrators, including chancellors, presidents, provosts, deans, and department chairpersons. All of their visits had been prepared by my own contact with the president of each institution, describing the purpose of the study and our interest in sending Goodwin and Nacht. Almost without exception, the campus responses were very positive, and many individuals then worked directly with the authors to make arrangements. The authors met over breakfast, lunch, and dinner, in seminar rooms and less formal meetings. In very few cases they met with only one individual. In most cases they met with five to ten faculty and administrators, and lively discussion ensued.

As the authors approached each campus, they had a series of questions that would help guide the discussion, but they were not bound by them. They encouraged everyone to speak freely and

Helen Cunningham, formerly program officer with the Trusts, a strong believer in the importance of this study and very helpful in the early stages of development. The dozens of colleges and universities who welcomed the authors and the individuals who facilitated their visits are too numerous to mention by name, but collectively they were essential to this effort and we owe them special thanks. Several individuals read the manuscript in early stages and offered especially helpful critique. They included Humphrey Tonkin, University of Hartford; Barbara Burn, University of Massachusetts; Pamela George, North Carolina Central University; and Elinor Barber, formerly at the Institute of International Education.

I also wish to express my personal appreciation to Craufurd Goodwin and Michael Nacht, who have contributed so generously of their time to the ongoing discussion of these issues long after they have completed the study. Through their lively and informed presentations they have already engaged the attention of many as to the importance of the issues raised in their report.

Cassandra A. Pyle
Executive Director
Council for International Exchange
of Scholars

Contents

Introduction

For many faculty the desire and the need to go abroad are inherent in the nature of their discipline, and for centuries scholars have traveled far and wide for academic purposes. For other faculty the thought of going abroad for scholarly purposes is completely alien. For many, however, the possibility of time abroad is simply not feasible, for a variety of personal considerations and a multitude of other reasons. To ask faculty whether they would go abroad for academic purposes generates many responses, often conflicting, that reveal the complexity of the role of international experience in their professional careers.

The Council for International Exchange of Scholars (CIES) has played a unique role in the more than forty years that it has worked with the Fulbright Scholar Program. We have sought to attract faculty for Fulbright research grants and lectureships, originally in a handful of countries; today we send approximately one thousand U.S. faculty abroad annually to more than 120 countries. Unlike most other programs supporting scholarly activity abroad, a high percentage of Fulbright grants for faculty are for overseas lecturing opportunities, and CIES has been keenly aware of the obstacles scholars face in going abroad in this capacity. However, all other distinguished fellowship programs for overseas research, as well as U.S. Agency for International Development (AID) funded technical assistance initiatives and campus-based programs that offer opportunities for faculty, have had difficulties attracting applicants at one time or another.

On the one hand, faculty mobility seems more pronounced, but on the other, we have seen clear signs of intransigence, unwillingness, or inability to go abroad. We have understandably wanted to know more about the international experience of faculty and to understand why so many face obstacles in going abroad or, upon return, encounter little recognition for their experience. At a time when our colleges and universities are espousing the importance of developing a strong international dimension and are reinstating language and international studies courses, it is baffling to us that so many faculty are not attracted to spending one or two terms abroad. Wherein lies the incentive, and what are the obstacles?

With the generous support of The Pew Charitable Trusts, CIES has been able to undertake a study of the international experience of faculty. We were fortunate that Craufurd Goodwin and Michael Nacht, who had already completed four studies on international education issues, agreed to take on this project. Goodwin and Nacht are both internationalists in their academic specialties, and both have held administrative positions within their institutions. Thus, they combined an academic and international perspective, coupled with a good working knowledge of university administration. Their recent studies on international education, begun in 1982, gave them particular insight into student exchange issues, including the relationship of faculty to these activities. All of these studies have been hailed as important instruments to generate reflection and dialogue. They have prepared provocative and analytical essays on topics relevant to policy-making committees, rather than statistically based studies for the scholarly community. It is this same type of approach that CIES chose to use in addressing the topic of the international experience of U.S. faculty.

We asked Goodwin and Nacht to undertake a study that would better inform us on the international experience of U.S. faculty. The questions to be posed were these: What type of U.S. faculty go abroad, and for what reasons? What are the incentives and disincentives for these sojourns? What trends are discernible in faculty experience abroad? What are the attitudes prevalent on U.S. campuses toward such activities? What are the special obstacles and risks faced by faculty who commit themselves to an international experience? What are the effects of foreign experi-

MISSING THE BOAT

For many faculty the desire and need to go abroad are inherent in
the nature of their discipline. For others the thought of going
abroad for scholarly purposes is completely alien. This book,
which was sponsored by the Council for International Exchange
of Scholars, looks in depth at the international experience of
American faculty. Goodwin and Nacht examine the type of faculty who go abroad and their reasons for doing so, the incentives
and disincentives for faculty travel abroad, the attitudes prevalent on U.S. campuses toward such activities, the special obstacles and risks faced by faculty who commit themselves to an international experience, and the effects of foreign experience
among the faculty on the internationalization of U.S. campuses.
In preparing the book, the authors conducted extensive interviews with faculty at thirty-seven institutions of higher education.

1

Higher education looks abroad: historical trends

Postgraduate training and the grand tour

Faculty members in U.S. colleges and universities have ventured overseas from the very earliest days.* As leaders of a colonial culture, they looked back to their metropolitan heartland for direction. Later, within an adolescent new community they turned still to the Old World for intellectual training, leadership, standards, and inspiration. They went back not only to Britain in search of roots, but to the continent as well for the experience of postgraduate training and a breadth of contacts appropriate to a young developing nation. Continental Europe remained the destination of most itinerant U.S. scholars throughout the nineteenth century. The main exceptions were clerics who set out for mission stations in Asia and Africa or the Holy Land. A few "orientalists" brought back reports from the mysterious East, but mainly in the form of travelers' tales and stories from exotic lands rather than as serious scholarly studies. The dominant posture of these early U.S. scholars abroad was often respectful humility toward their elders and betters; they came primarily to watch and to learn and, except for the missionaries to the heathen, seldom to teach or to contribute. Some of the expatriates were even openly contemptuous and ashamed of the society they left behind, and they apologized for the philistine ways of those who stayed at

* An excellent account of the internationalization of U.S. institutions is Robert McCaughey, *International Studies and Academic Enterprise* (New York: Columbia University Press, 1984).

1

home. Scholarly travel was for practical reasons the preserve principally of those with private wealth, and to some degree the study tour of young Americans became associated, in fact and in public perception, with the continental grand tour of young British aristocrats.

Undoubtedly a condition limiting the amount of international travel by U.S. academics in the nineteenth century was an overall sense of the continental vastness of North America and the need to deal with local problems of nation building before taking on the world. The Monroe Doctrine, which confined the United States politically to its own hemisphere, had its less formal cultural counterpart.

From the late nineteenth century on, the main change in the demeanor of U.S. scholars overseas was a growing self-confidence and reduced deference toward their foreign mentors. They continued to travel to the principal academic centers of Germany, France, Austria, or the United Kingdom for advanced training and continued stimulation, but they did so now with the knowledge that they could return to burgeoning research programs at Johns Hopkins, Chicago, Cornell, Wisconsin, Berkeley, and the like. Edwin Gay, who studied economic history at Berlin with Gustav Schmoller and then returned to become the first dean of the Harvard Business School, and who was a major force in the formation of the Council on Foreign Relations, typifies these early transatlantic scholars. John Bates Clark in economics and James T. Shotwell in history and international relations were in the front ranks of their disciplines.

The watershed of war

World War I and to a far greater extent World War II drew U.S. faculty overseas and into the examination of international affairs as never before. It was partly that military and war-related service took them abroad and internationalized them willy-nilly. International travel became a familiar experience for those who had barely thought of going beyond the county seat before the Great War. But in addition, the war raised for the United States the

prospect of new global opportunities and responsibilities as old empires crumbled. The demonstrated unpreparedness of the United States to comprehend the process of which it was a part, both during World War I and at the Peace Conference afterward, suggested to many young Americans the need both to understand other countries better and to reflect on different ways to arrange relations among states. The study of international relations increased in the United States between the wars, with practitioners lodged both in universities and in nongovernmental research institutions like the Council on Foreign Relations, the Carnegie Endowment for International Peace, and the Brookings Institution. The globe-trotting academic peace seeker of this period was typified by the indefatigable Nicholas Murray Butler, president both of Columbia University and the Carnegie Endowment for International Peace.

World War II added far more to the international experience of U.S. scholars than had its predecessor. In this case the conflict brought young Americans to Asia and the Middle East, as well as to Europe. Academics were involved not only in military service but also in intelligence, logistical planning, and, after the war, occupation and recovery. For the first time many of these scholars were faced squarely with the necessity to understand the languages and cultures of both friend and foe and to comprehend the nature of past and potential global systems. No matter whether engineer or economist in their scholarly lives, while on national service they were required to learn about Japanese and German societies, first to defeat the nations in battle and then to think about rebuilding them. If they were going to fight beside the Chinese and the Poles, they had better understand them as well. As the Russians shifted quickly from being allies to adversaries in the years after World War II, they became a special enigma. Consider, for example, that there was no university-based Soviet and Russian studies research center in the United States until 1946. As a consequence of the war, the rest of the world became to U.S. higher education not simply a source of wisdom and an object of cultural curiosity, but a subject of responsibility as well. If the United States was indeed required, as seemed to be the case, to put the world back together under the United Nations and other multilateral organizations, and if it was required also, as seemed likely by the late 1940s, to lead the countries of the "free world" against the forces of darkness, it was no longer a luxury, but a necessity, to travel the globe to master all of its intricacies. The old European empires had often been the subject of contempt among U.S. scholars, and finally they were now on their last legs. But if it was to be the United States' role to put new systems in their place, the crumbling imperial structures had to be fully understood and the alternatives carefully crafted.

New styles of academic travel

The kinds of U.S. academic travelers that emerged from the shambles of World War II were in most cases quite different from those who came before. The international relations specialists were almost the only element of continuity. Having moved on from faith in the old League of Nations and World Court, they were devoted now to the strengthening of new international mechanisms, from the United Nations and its component organizations through the North Atlantic Treaty Organization and the General Agreement on Tariffs and Trade to the European Economic Community. They found common cause with scholars in other countries and they traveled widely to sustain contacts and master institutional detail. Some of them became committed to a "realist" approach based on power politics that was stressed by Hans Morgenthau and Arnold Wolfers, leaving behind the emphasis on collective security that had its roots in the writings and deeds of Woodrow Wilson.

With most of the great cities in ruins, for a time at least, U.S. scholars after the war did not have a well-established travel path. Furthermore, the massive migration of intellectuals from Europe to the United States just before the war had substantially eviscerated most of the great European university centers, and there was no longer the need to sit at the feet of a far-off master. The master now was likely to be at Princeton, Chicago, or MIT. As one physicist said to us, "In the 1920s we went to Göttingen; then we brought Göttingen here."

At least five new categories of academic traveler emerged in the postwar years to take the place of the now obsolete categories of grand tourister and scholarly apprentice. The first consisted of participants in reconstruction and development assistance programs. Starting with the administration of occupations in Europe and Japan and continuing through President Harry Truman's Point Four Program, the Marshall Plan, and various development assistance initiatives culminating in the establishment of the U.S. Agency for International Development (AID) and the Peace Corps, U.S. academics were used in the rehabilitation and development of countries in all regions of the world. They served in the multilateral assistance agencies of the United Nations (the World Health Organization, the Food and Agriculture Organization, etc.) as well as in U.S. governmental programs. Scholars were appointed in those programs not only as advisers and administrators, but as top-level planners and leaders. The American academic world became well populated with professors who one day were in the corn fields of Nebraska and on the next were reconstructing German industry, implanting democracy in Japan, seeking to improve the rice crop in the Philippines, or rethinking the urban design of Calcutta. Those were heady days indeed. Although it seemed probable in the early years after the war that this category of "recovery and development academic" would disappear with the completion of the economic rebirth of the war-devastated nations, it was in fact sustained by U.S. acceptance of continuing responsibility for assistance to developing new nations.

The second new category of traveling scholar was made up of "area studies" specialists committed to gaining a better understanding of a particular country or region of the world. In some cases area specialists were refugees from the region in question, particularly in the case of countries "behind the Iron Curtain." In other cases they were native-born Americans who received their first training in foreign lands during the occupation or in intelligence and other war-related government employment. Back in universities they simply continued to do what came naturally. In still other cases area studies specialists were scholars committed to the comparative method who sought in foreign countries varied data about human behavior and institutions that would lead to generalized truths. The growth of area studies in the postwar years was a financial and intellectual roller-coaster, with the programs both of private foundations and public agencies reflecting shifts in philanthropic fashion and in world events. Successes in the Soviet space program in the late 1950s – especially the launching of the first earth-orbiting satellite, *Sputnik,* in October 1957 – are generally credited with causing an almost hysterical rush to improve U.S. levels of understanding in science, as well as in foreign area studies. As a consequence, in the late 1950s and 1960s major grant programs of The Ford Foundation and the federal government (under the National Defense Education Act) provided substantial funding for the establishment of numerous foreign language and area studies programs and centers on U.S. college and university campuses. Although initially well supported, these centers suffered from being interdisciplinary anomalies in discipline-oriented U.S. universities. One of the results of this development of well-defined communities of specialists on most areas of the world was an informal *credentialing process* for scholarly travel to those areas. Serious students of a country or region were henceforth expected to come equipped with linguistic and cultural expertise, normally certified by receipt of an advanced degree from one of the recognized university training centers. Area study specialists, then, took on a paradoxical role with respect to travel within "their" areas. On the one hand, they were zealous advocates of experiences gained in an approved fashion; on the other hand, they were dubious of, or even hostile to, any less rigorous approaches.

The third style of academic overseas experience grew out of an idealistic sense that the world would be a better place if only people at all levels knew much more about each other and jettisoned old prejudices and stereotypes. In the broadest interpretation for the average citizen this idealism was represented in the people-to-people programs started during the Eisenhower years. Among high school students it found expression in several programs: the American Field Service, the Experiment in International Living, and Youth for Understanding. For college and university teachers the main funder in this mode became the Fulbright Scholar Program (1946), which reflected the idealism of its sponsor, Senator J. William Fulbright of Arkansas.

The fourth route to academic travel was through what came to be called cultural diplomacy or public diplomacy. The agents of U.S. foreign policy employed as minor weapons in their diplomatic arsenals the activities of academics overseas. Various travel programs of the United States Information Agency (USIA), together with some in the departments of State and Defense, fit in this category. The Peace Corps, although having motives larger than these other programs and including relatively few academics, is nevertheless in the same genre. With the breakdown of a consensus in U.S. foreign policy, especially following recriminations about policies in Africa, Southeast Asia and Latin America, these programs lost some appeal for academics, and scholarship and public diplomacy have tended to go their separate ways.

Fifth and finally, in the years after World War II there continued to be a core of academics who ventured abroad because their disciplines or subdisciplines demanded it: to gather historical and cultural data, collect geological or biological materials, assess works of art, enhance language competency, or perform some other well-defined task. This core has grown steadily with the size of the higher education sector. All of these categories as they exist today are discussed in the chapters that follow.

From colony to empire and back to something in between

Views of the world in U.S. higher education were transformed almost overnight by World War II. From a cultural colony the nation was changed, at least in its own eyes, into the metropolis; from the periphery it moved triumphantly to the center. After all, it was helping to create a United States of Europe, democracy in

Japan, and new nations out of former colonial appendages. In retrospect we can see that the United States may not in fact have become a true imperial power during this period, but in many ways it behaved as if it had. The worldwide scholarly community came to be seen by U.S. scholars as needing help and deserving to be tended, both from a sense of *noblesse obliqe* and because so doing would strengthen the Western Alliance at the same time. Just as Britain and France in earlier years had viewed their colonial educational systems sympathetically but patronizingly, so scholars in the United States after World War II could hardly conceive of the rest of the world in more than a derivative role, except perhaps when students they had trained performed some clever extensions of practices learned in the United States. U.S. scholars, in effect, reflected the intellectual strength that flowed from an economy that in 1950 accounted for more than 50 percent of the world's gross product.

To some degree the increasing use of English as the language of scholarly discourse may have misled U.S. scholars about their place in the world and strengthened the notion of intellectual hegemony. While this device prospered largely as a convenience to facilitate communication, it was interpreted by some as evidence of U.S. cultural dominance and an irresistible tendency toward global homogenization on the United States model. If the people of other nations are looking more and more like us, the thinking ran, why pay attention to their current languages and cultural peculiarities?

The rapid development of an imperial mentality within U.S. universities may have been accelerated by the growth of what was called in the 1960s the "multiversity." This term in fact concealed the enfeeblement of central authority within the university and the rise of the independent entrepreneur, whether dean, department chairman, institute director, or ambitious professor, as key decision maker. In the "multiversity" the imperial mentality could persist in some of the constituent units long after it was no longer relevant on the larger stage and had degenerated into mere provincialism. The celebrated Harvard principle of "each tub" within the institution "on its own bottom," inherent in the concept of the "multiversity," relieved the central leadership not only of considerable responsibility, but also of much of its capacity to shape events. Presidential rhetoric in the "multiversity" was assumed to be empty. And university presidents were ill equipped to lead the community of scholars into a postimperial era. Not every U.S. university by the 1960s, of course, was a "multiversity." Effective central leadership and a strong sense of community prevailed in many places. But as a model toward which some institutions seemed to be moving, the concept was illuminating.

The United States' period of overwhelming political and economic dominance of the world scene, the twentieth-century equivalent of imperial control, lasted less than a quarter of a century. Certainly by the 1970s the rise of other economic centers, notably Western Europe and Japan, which was indeed encouraged by U.S. foreign policy, destroyed all dreams of continued economic hegemony. The debacle in Vietnam and increasing independence among former client states also put to rest the conception of a unified collection of free world nations gathered under the U.S. petticoats, as it were, against the threat of totalitarian aggression.

The 1970s and 1980s have been taken up largely with attempts by the United States to come to grips with its (in relative terms) diminished economic and political power, from the Smithsonian Declaration disclaiming the previous degree of international economic responsibility, to the growing acceptance of German strength in NATO, to the devouring among the intellectual elite of Paul Kennedy's *The Rise and Fall of the Great Powers*.

This study of international travel of U.S. faculty is concerned very largely with comparable attempts in the United States to adjust intellectually and institutionally to a changing world. The focus is on the overseas experience of U.S. faculty and attitudes toward it, but to a very large degree this experience and these attitudes are merely a reflection of the deeper adjustment, or lack thereof, that is taking place throughout the country to a world marked by increasing complexity, the decline of U.S. authority, and a plethora of economic, political, and military centers of power. U.S. scholarly hegemony may have persisted slightly longer than the country's economic and political dominance, but the directions of change are undoubtedly the same. Clearly the capacity of the U.S. higher educational community to recognize this change and adapt thereto may be as significant as the nation's response in other segments of its affairs. We return to these broader issues in the final chapter.

2

Who goes today?
and who does not?

In this chapter we identify and discuss categories of faculty who
went abroad, and those who did not, from the United States in the
late 1980s. This categorization is based on detailed discussions
with upwards of a thousand persons on U.S. campuses. The fine-
ness of grain selected for the categories is a matter of taste; the
main criterion is that the categories be usefully distinct. There are
various ways to go about the categorization. For example, a case
can be made for an organizing distinction based upon experiences
devoted to, respectively, the three legs of the stool of faculty
responsibility: teaching, research, and service. Faculty do, indeed, go abroad for all three of these purposes. We choose instead, however, a first cut based on whether an overseas experience is aimed at professional or personal gain, recognizing, of
course, that the two objectives may sometimes be tied together.
We discern five categories of those who go abroad with a professional mission. We also find six subcategories of faculty who
cannot or do not by choice go abroad for extended periods at all.
We hope we provide enough illustrative detail to make this taxon-
omy both comprehensible and useful.

We became very aware during our explorations that certain
background characteristics lying behind all of these categories
tend to predetermine the disposition of faculty for an overseas
experience. In particular prior foreign travel seems a significant
determinant of subsequent interest. We found those with past
service overseas in the Peace Corps, church missions, and even
the military most eager to take the plunge again. More vague than

the force of these experiences but just as important, we suspect, is the adventurous spirit present or absent in a scholar. Those with this spirit, no matter in which category they rested, were most likely to pack their bags and go. "You have to be a romantic to go abroad for an extended period," we were told by one humanist in the Pacific Northwest, and we suspect she is right.

Area studies

By far the most conspicuous U.S. international academic travelers since the end of World War II have been the specialists on foreign areas, especially those on "less familiar" parts of the world in Asia, Africa, and Latin America. Most were trained during the palmy days of bountiful public and private support in the 1950s, 1960s, and early 1970s. We had confidently expected them to be the most pathetic and mistreated of our categories, left high and dry by the shifts of fashion and decline in funding and unable any longer to get back to the foreign raw material from which they draw nourishment. Nothing could be farther from the truth. With very few exceptions the area specialists with whom we met were remarkably upbeat. They return to their regions often and seemingly with relatively little difficulty. They feel that really there is no choice for them; either they renew their exposure to their countries regularly or they perish as scholars. Accordingly they have learned to hustle and to find the support somewhere. Their knowledge of the societies in which they work has also enabled them to arrange visits more cheaply than newcomers. Almost none with whom we spoke, in small college or major university alike, working on Asia, Africa, or Latin America, reported insurmountable problems in finding the necessary funding to go abroad. Virtually all said they had invariably to use imagination, but they got there and survived one way or another. The area specialists have a strong sense of confidence in the merit of what they are doing and the possibility of carrying it through. This is part of the culture they acquired in their graduate training. They saw their mentors engaged in the ceaseless search for funding to get to the field, and they imbibed the sharp sense of the necessity to follow suit, as well as how to do it to succeed. For them, to go abroad is legitimate and essential. By and large, they learned the funding sources and the application techniques, and perhaps most important, they acquired the chutzpah to keep trying when rebuffed. One young area specialist reported that he had consistently experienced only a 40 percent success rate in applications over a decade. But he expected this and was not discouraged. Another calculated that thus far in his career he had applied for a total of $120,000 in travel support and had received $60,000. Frequently we met area specialists who pieced together support for their field work from several sources, such as overseas teaching, consulting, and grants for conference travel from their home institutions. One East Asian specialist, who told us that he had arranged to spend at least two months in his country every year since leaving graduate school in the early 1970s, was typical. We caught him departing on a Fulbright; in prior years he had had grants from the National Endowment for the Humanities and the American Council of Learned Societies.

We asked one grizzled anthropologist area specialist for a list off the top of his head of where he had sought support for his field work over the course of his career, and he offered the following: National Science Foundation, National Institutes of Health, U.S. Agency for International Development, United Nations Development Program, North Atlantic Treaty Organization, International Development Research Center (Canada), United States Information Agency, the Fulbright Program, the Ford, Rockefeller, and Wenner Gren Foundations, the World Bank, the developmental agencies of several foreign countries, and travel funds at his own university. He was committed to finding more sources if need be.

An illuminating contrast to the credentialed area specialists are the prospective newcomers to foreign area studies attempting to break in at midcareer. They complain vigorously about absence of support; usually they have little familarity with sources and often they lack the self-confidence and the contacts to persevere. Moreover, they speculate that credentialed area specialists dominate the selection panels, thereby reducing appreciably the likelihood of their own success.

In general the area studies category of academic travelers is committed unconditionally to continued foreign exposure. One told us he felt seriously deprived if compelled to remain in the United States uninterruptedly even for as long as twelve months! His teaching, his research, and his psychic welfare are all dependent on periodic cross-cultural infusions. That is not to say we did not hear complaints from area specialists about the grantsmanship process. Some deplored the effects of politics and fashion on funding for various areas; others said that their need always to "wing it" made them feel marginalized in relation to more secure areas of scholarship such as the natural sciences. But when all was said and done, they still were prepared to make do and get wherever they needed to go.

We did not explore the adequacy of funds for graduate students to conduct field research overseas and therefore were not able to ascertain whether the pipeline of new area studies specialists remains full.

Study abroad programs for students

The 1970s and even more the 1980s have brought an explosion of interest in study abroad among students on the U.S. campus. In prior decades overseas experience had been confined mainly either to juniors at elite liberal arts colleges or to language majors aiming to improve their linguistic facility. In those earlier times, program directors were typically language or history instructors – faculty who were already intimately familiar with the countries to which they led their charges. A major difference in more recent study abroad programs is that they are spread widely throughout the courses of study and parts of the institution, from freshman year to advanced graduate training and from the undergraduate college to some graduate and professional schools. They can be found in all kinds of institutions, from the community college to the high-powered technical research university, in institutions that are public and private, rural and urban, secular and church related. A particular characteristic of the newer study abroad program is that often the leader knows little more than the students about the place where they settle. Study abroad, then, becomes a mind-expanding experience for the leader as well as for the led.*

Some of the new-model study abroad leaders are faculty members who fall comfortably in one of the other categories in this list. They are area studies specialists, natural scientists, and social scientists seeking research materials, or they are using this device to acquire a ticket overseas for miscellaneous purposes. We met faculty who used the opportunity of study abroad to pursue their teaching and research interests in subjects as diverse as filmmaking, jazz festivals, and Japanese religion. But all are not this well focused. Many are either attracted to the novelty of teaching overseas or are dragooned by administrators desperate for warm leadership bodies. Undoubtedly U.S. study abroad leaders number overall in the thousands each year. The effects of study abroad on the leaders themselves are seldom taken into account by institutional administrators when developing the programs, but often they are great. We heard numerous tales from study abroad veterans of career changes, research stimulation, teaching reinvigoration, and personal regeneration. (One professional from the Pacific Northwest stated that to conduct research while overseeing a study abroad program requires careful planning, including finding a place to live at least two bus stops from the closest student!) We left these discussions with the strong sense that oversees programs for students, perhaps combined with other devices, remain one of the most promising unexploited and even unexplored devices to provide U.S. faculty with the benefits of an international experience described below. This is certainly one of the most obvious means to recruit the recalcitrant and to reap the benefits of serendipity. Moreover it provides access to a source of travel funds. A natural objective could be, perhaps, to make possible the greatest gain to faculty from these experiences by providing for collateral or sequential research opportunities and other enrichments, recognizing that travel and

---

* As noted in the introduction, these findings are examined at length in the authors' previous work, *Abroad and Beyond: Patterns in American Overseas Education* (New York: Cambridge University Press, 1988).

set-up costs are already in place. If a study abroad director and family are already ensconced abroad, a period of time devoted to the faculty member's enrichment at the conclusion of the directorial responsibility can be purchased at low marginal cost.

The benefits to faculty of study abroad teaching and direction vary greatly across fields and among individuals. Only the most disciplined scholar can undertake a substantial research project while part of an overseas program for students. But some do, especially those who are old hands at both the research and the programs. Moreover, faculty can benefit in many other ways, in particular by maintaining continuing contact with changing conditions in the country and with scholarly colleagues. For example we met a professor of comparative Asian religions who kept up-to-date by effectively tacking three-week research periods onto the ends of study abroad tours in various Asian locations. He admitted that he was not a high-powered scholar likely to qualify repeatedly for overseas research awards; nevertheless he was able regularly to invigorate his teaching by resorting to participation in a study abroad program. Obviously a professor of solid state physics could not pursue this strategy as effectively. But opportunities exist for many more experiments in this direction.

A quick response of many faculty to the notion of combining research or other forms of enrichment with the leadership of study abroad was that little else could be accomplished by program directors beyond ministering to their charges. But we heard enough examples to the contrary, where participation in study abroad had indeed become the mechanism for sustaining international competence, that we were persuaded that multiple accomplishment was possible. It seems also that the side benefits of faculty participation in study abroad programs may not always be readily apparent to those who are benefiting while caught up in the hurly-burly of administration in foreign cities. The benefits are more easily observable with hindsight or through the eyes of outside observers.

Development assistance

Much of the assistance channeled by the United States to the developing world since World War II has passed through American universities, particularly the public land-grant institutions. The reason is obvious; these suppliers have what the demanders want: technical assistance and advanced training in practical subjects related to economic development. The great land-grant institutions of the country have supplied agricultural experts, foresters, engineers, teachers of education, and specialists in innumerable other applied fields. They do this for a variety of reasons rooted in their perception of their self-interest. One veteran of the process suggested to us that the main stimuli were "overhead, competition from their peers, and altruism – in that order."

The reasons for U.S. foreign aid can be found mainly in foreign policy: Objectives include the provision of rewards to allies, containment of the spread of communism, and help to the poor and suffering. President John F. Kennedy's exhortation of his fellow Americans to help the developing nations to "help themselves" was as deeply rooted in U.S. national security objectives as it was in humanitarian impulses. Effects of foreign assistance contracts on university recipients were considered only incidentally by the federal grant agencies and then mainly with respect to the universities' capacity to be efficiently responsive in the future. However, a very significant, even though unintended, side effect of these contracts has been to internationalize and deprovincialize the institutions. It is truly remarkable to visit one of the major land-grant universities today and find a cosmopolitan faculty and administration, often surpassing in sophistication the older and more liberal arts-oriented sister institutions in the state. We met professors of range science and irrigation engineering who seemed substantially more self-confident about and conscious of the world than their presumably more internationalist historian and linguistic brethren down the road. At one large state university that we visited we were told that typically between forty and sixty faculty are serving abroad at any one time. Some of these are on long-term assignment, perhaps appointed specifically for this purpose and acting almost as a private colonial service. But many are from the regular faculty, cycling through the development assistance process, being shaped and molded thereby, and influencing their students accordingly.

Even though U.S. foreign assistance programs have not had as one of their objectives to internationalize a part of America, this has been their effect. And perhaps this result should be kept in mind when consideration is given to sustaining or terminating, forming or reforming, these programs. A recognition of this complex domestic result of development assistance programs might lead to beneficial modifications that would make them even more valuable. One of the insistent appeals we heard on the land-grant campuses was for more flexible and short-term contracts for senior faculty so that they could continue development links into their later years. Another suggestion was for closer contacts with the liberal arts departments on campuses so that international studies could be coordinated more effectively with development assistance. One of the hazards of establishing separate and isolated development assistance cadres on campuses is reputed to be their permanent seduction away from the scholarly life. Overall, however, we came away convinced that university-based development assistance was a "positive sum game" for all concerned: It aided the developing country, it enhanced the professional competence of faculty members, and it internationalized the universities from which the faculty members came.

"International" disciplines and subdisciplines

Apart from area studies, where the focus of scholars is mainly on a single country or region of the world, there are certain academic disciplines and parts of disciplines (subdisciplines) that are also avowedly international and therefore see repeated international experiences as essential to their health and growth. These disciplines and subdisciplines, in turn, fall into two subcategories.

The first subcategory contains those subjects that by their essence require materials, data, or specific experiences that can be found only overseas. This includes, for example, linguistics, geology, literature, anthropology, biology, architecture, soil science, and music and art history. In all of these disciplines, and others like them, it is unusual for graduate students, as it is for senior faculty, not to spend considerable time abroad, talking to subjects, collecting specimens, digging rocks, admiring buildings and urban settings, or absorbing works of art that look very different from their appearance in books or slides when seen in place.

To probe just one such discipline in a little depth, we spoke at length with several professors of architecture. They told us that specialists in architecture or design today simply cannot be first class if they are parochial and have not traveled abroad extensively. Understanding the cultural dimension is crucial to successful architecture, and life-style differences must be experienced. The architect or designer must observe the relationships between human values and urban structures, and these can be appreciated best in comparative perspective.

The requirements differ for individual scholars, of course, but in general it is not essential for most of the travelers in these international disciplines and subdisciplines either to drink deeply at the springs of local culture or to immerse themselves in the foreign academic community for extended periods. Their objectives are simple: The rest of the world has "things" that they require, whether rocks or a view of a sculpture, and they need only to go and get them. Some disciplines, notably the social sciences, have parts or subdisciplines that do require sustained international exposure, for example, comparative economic systems, comparative government, and European history. They are the exceptions in this first category.

The second category of international disciplines and subdisciplines contains a miscellany of applied subjects and fields that have decided they require an international dimension to be meaningful and to reach fulfillment. Some of these arrived at this conclusion for obvious reasons, others for less obvious ones. The most striking example on our visits was business administration. There, the national accrediting body, the American Assembly of Collegiate Schools of Business (AACSB), has mandated the cultivation of an international dimension, and around the country we encountered schools struggling mightily to comply. Historically the special field of "international business" has been treated as a poor stepchild in business school curricula, especially in comparison to mainstream fields like marketing and finance. The current move is intended, not to perpetuate this segregated focus, but to internationalize the entire discipline root and branch. In most cases the schools recognize that providing their faculty the direct experience of another economy is the most promising first step to internationalizing the curriculum and research program. Indeed, at one of the United States' most prestigious graduate schools of business we were informed that the dean deliberately sought to cultivate overseas teaching opportunities for his faculty as a subtle means of internationalizing what had been a startlingly parochial U.S.-based curriculum.

We heard about a wide range of devices to achieve the genuine internationalization of business schools, including heavy subsidies to foreign research, negotiation of attractive exchange relationships with foreign business schools, and even opening branches overseas. The most serious obstacle faced by the leaders of business schools in luring their faculty overseas was the high personal opportunity cost incurred by these faculty. Many business school teachers have lucrative consulting activities that cease when they leave the country. On our visits we met only a few seasoned world travelers in the business schools who had spent extensive periods abroad. There were, however, growing numbers of faculty who had spent brief periods, at least, overseas. A large question faced by business schools, as by other applied programs, remains whether to internationalize through several designated internationalists located in a separate department or division or to do so by infusing an international perspective throughout the school. Nonetheless, the consensus seems to be shifting toward greater international perspectives across the faculty, which implies the need for widely distributed international experience.

It was obvious why business schools were mounting a drive toward internationalization, with rising foreign trade and investment all around them. It was less clear how some other applied fields had reached the decision to internationalize, laudable as this might be. In the case of schools of education it was suggested that teachers needed to understand both a pluralistic world, in order to instruct better, and foreign methods so as to reform our own unsatisfactory educational techniques. We heard essentially the same case made by both faculty and administrators for library science, public administration, social work, home economics, and other applied fields.

The professional schools that appeared most likely to follow business schools in a rush to internationalize were schools of theology. Once again, external agencies seemed the main stimulus for change. At one divinity school we were told the supporting church was shifting funds from missionary work to internationalization of the clergy. Lacking other ready means at hand, the leaders of most of the applied areas with a concern to internationalize were taking advantage of the enthusiasm of their students and were seeking to infect their faculty with an international virus by involving them in some kind of study abroad. Curiously it seemed sometimes that a few visionary deans were in league with students, who perceived their future on a global stage, to pull along recalcitrant and conservative faculty.

The sciences

We found the sciences to be the most complex and most challenging of our categories to sort out and understand. Here, as in some other parts of this subject, it was very difficult to distinguish reality from rhetoric. Once again, it is helpful to propose several subcategories of reasons why scientists go abroad.

1. Field work

Parts of many scientific disciplines have particular needs to gather specialized materials overseas. Some disciplines like geology and anthropology depend entirely on international data. Plant geneticists, but not all botanists, must go overseas for germ plasm; some, but not all, epidemiologists must follow their diseases overseas; and volcanologists go to their eruptions. By and large we found scientists conducting this kind of field work not deeply affected by the "international" nature of the experience required of them. It just involves the complication of a passport and a longer plane ride. As one remarked to us, he might as well be "going to Wyoming." The local culture and even the language are minor impediments to these scientists, but seldom enough to justify the expenditure of effort sufficient to understand them fully.

2. Collaboration and machines

Another subcategory of scientists looks to the rest of the world for particular persons with whom to study and collaborate or for particular laboratories with specialized instrumentation in which to work. A most obvious example in this category is the high-energy physics laboratory at CERN in Switzerland. But increasingly there are other specialized facilities of exceptional interest to U.S. scientists, a centrifuge here, a telescope there. Often there are specialized financial resources as well, either U.S. or foreign, that enable elite members of the various scientific communities to come together at these facilities and pool their intellects.

As in the case of the foreign field workers in the prior category, however, there is not a great deal of "foreignness" in the time spent overseas by these scientists. The language used on site is almost invariably English, and the attitude of many U.S. scientists is that the people and facilities are substantially the by-products and extensions of science in the United States. The U.S. attitude is a little like that of English visitors to Boston in the nineteenth century, who found it was nice to see the colonies growing up!

Most of those who venture abroad for conventional scientific reasons do so with support from the large public funding agencies. A significant number, however, also made use of consulting support from the private sector. For example, a chemist or a micro-biologist may visit a foreign laboratory to explore a process or a product interesting to a U.S. firm. Indeed as the rest of the world catches up with and sometimes surpasses the United States in more and more areas of applied science, we expect industrial and commercial assistance in support of foreign visits and collaboration to become an increasingly significant source of travel dollars. Scholars will become, in effect, part of a front-line intelligence service in the battle for economic competitiveness and markets.

3. Recharging the batteries

Midcareer burn-out is a familiar phenomenon throughout academic life, and it is reported frequently by scientists, notably by theorists and often by particularly good ones. It may be the intensity of their early labors, the realization that their greatest achievements are behind them, or the growing intolerability and intolerance of their colleagues that leads them simply to have to get away. A sojourn overseas seems to provide an effective intellectual catharsis for scientists in this category. The typical pattern is to attach oneself rather loosely to an overseas institution of high quality in one's field and to spend time there talking and thinking in an unstructured fashion. This mode is clearly different from the CERN collaboration described above, but it may be just as important for the progress of science. The veterans of this refresher experience could not explain precisely what had transpired on their visits. All they knew was that they returned home reborn and reinvigorated emotionally and intellectually. One said, only half in jest, that the good food and opera he had enjoyed were essential catalysts for the intellectual process that occurred. We suggest the phenomenon is no less significant for its inexplicability. We asked repeatedly, "Couldn't you have had the same results at Chicago or Berkeley?" and the answer typically was "Probably not. That would be too much like home." Scientists we met in this category were theoretical physicists, mathematicians, astronomers, and others who could spend an extended period away from the home base productively, with not much more equipment than a pen and pencil. Because of the unfocused nature of this experience scientists must fund it usually from sabbatical pay or some other kind of internal paid leave, rather than from an external source.

4. Getting the answers overseas

Undoubtedly the most fascinating subcategory of U.S. scientists proceeding overseas in growing numbers includes those in some areas of applied science who believe they absolutely must go because that is where the scientific action is. They believe that their foreign counterparts are not merely catching up, but have passed the United States and are now out ahead, alone on the scientific frontier. In the other subcategories of traveling scientist, discussed above, the contextual challenge is perceived as minimal or nonexistent. Although we were told repeatedly by persons representing the other subcategories that the culture of science is universal (that is, there are no significant methodological differences among nations, and happily the language of science is English), we heard these generalizations categorically rejected by applied scientists.

In essence the perspectives of those in a variety of applied areas, such as aquaculture, robotics, superconductors, and parts of civil and mining engineering, are consistent and roughly as follows. First, they find that other countries have simply pulled up to and gone ahead of the United States in innumerable applications that are of great scientific and immense economic significance. Whether this is because comparative advantage has shifted, because the United States has been lamentably backward in support for research and development in applied areas, or because these countries have perceived payoff in some areas more astutely than has the United States is not clear. But the result is that other nations have leapt out in front, both in development of applications and in the understanding that lies behind these applications. Second, in these applied areas they have not followed the supposed universal culture of science. Often they do not publish results or even commit themselves to paper. And when they do, the language is their own, not English. The reward structure and intellectual style of applied scientists in these fields in other countries, we were told repeatedly, is conditioned by their various cultural environments and very often especially by the requirement of a short-term practical payoff. Research is conducted not in universities, but usually in government or corporate laboratories, or at least with government or corporate funding. Sponsors like these, with clear practical objectives in mind, to develop new products or techniques or improve old ones, are not interested in publications in English in the international literature. Indeed, to the contrary, such publication might alert and give advantage to competitors. Exposition of ideas for local consumption in working papers or research reports is quite enough.

The implication of this situation for the United States in applied science around the world is that access can be gained to the frontiers of scientific development only through a process of human interaction among scientists that is far more complex and demanding than the attendance at meetings and consultations with the English-language literature that are said to be all that is required at the moment in pure science. This process of scientific interaction may be exceptionally complicated where political tensions exist, as with the Soviet Union, although even here, difficulties have lagged considerably as a result of *glasnost*.

We heard enough accounts of how U.S. applied scientists are coping with these new conditions of foreign superiority in their fields to discern definite patterns. Two especially thought-provoking cases in different parts of the world and in different fields suggest uniformities. One case was in marine science, where Japanese scientists, working mainly in government laboratories, are way ahead of their U.S. counterparts in developing ways to cultivate and exploit the oceans. The other is mining technology, where mining corporations in South America are well ahead of the United States in techniques of extracting and processing ore. In both cases, if U.S. scientists do not keep up-to-date on what is happening in these other nations, they remain perpetually obsolete and concerned with reinventing wheels that are already turning in someone else's economy. The ever-advancing research frontier is firmly fixed in these other countries, and if Americans wish to operate in it, that is where they must go. An immediate question we asked of these two and other comparable cases was whether the foreign scientific communities are purposely secretive about their activities. The answer was that they are not, but at the same time they are not necessarily prepared to share information in a fashion that is agreeable to U.S. scientists. For example, an unfamiliar U.S. marine scientist or mining engineer air-dropped into Japan or Chile is unlikely to receive more than a polite cold shoulder. The natives are not implementing a security system; rather, they are very busy and can see no point in wasting time with some foreigner from whom they cannot obviously benefit and whose motives are not well understood.

The only approach that yields effective access in these cases is to establish over time with the foreign scientists a sense of community, familiarity, and cooperation for mutual benefit. This approach requires above all frequent exchange and the development of tolerance and understanding, including sympathy for the other culture and perhaps some attempt at least at language facility. For the two institutions that reported these cases there was perceived to be no real alternative to following this course. In both cases they told of a steady flow of students and faculty in both directions and of collaborative endeavors of various kinds, depending on the comparative advantages of the partners. Under these conditions they reported a full sharing of information and research findings. As one group leader told us, "If we didn't follow this course, we would be nowhere." These two cases were far from the only ones of the kind we encountered (for example, we heard an equally interesting account of interaction on fisheries research with the Soviet Union), but they are illustrative.

The aquaculture case might be thought of as an area of applied science where U.S. activities are simply small-scale compared to those of other nations and in which we must always depend on leaders elsewhere. Mining is a field where U.S. industry is extremely cyclical, and sustained attention to the subject comes naturally in more stable industries overseas. A third area of applied science deals with what were described to us as "mature and sclerotic" industries, such as construction. Although buildings, bridges, dams, power plants, and highways are still built in the United States in profusion, innovative approaches to their construction come increasingly from youthful overseas economies with which U.S. industry, civil engineering, and architecture must maintain close contact if they are to stay within sight of the future. Periodic rejuvenation must come from abroad. One professor of urban design told us that he used to go overseas to see "the monuments." Now he must leave the United States to "find where it's at."

Important questions are raised by the existence of this group of cases in the applied sciences:

(a) Is this a growing set? As the world economy evolves in size and complexity, can we expect the frontiers of applied science in many other areas to move outward to other countries?

(b) Is this subcategory likely before long to contain parts of pure as well as applied science, where it will be necessary for pure scientists to develop complex interrelationships and cultural sophistication, which they now think unnecessary?

(c) Is there a dangerous lag-time between the moment when a field moves into this subcategory and the time when the relevant community of U.S. scientists is able to respond to it? If so, is there a case for public intervention to encourage U.S. scientists to prepare themselves for the new conditions they may face? For example, if U.S. physicists and electrical engineers had maintained close links with their Japanese counterparts in the 1970s and 1980s, is it possible that today they would be better able to take advantage of the superconductor revolution wrought in Japan?

(d) Finally, if the complex cultural relations of applied scientists (and potentially of pure scientists as well) are crucial for scientific advance in the years ahead, are the mechanisms in place to facilitate this development? Can we count any longer on the imaginative makeshift entrepreneurship of the scientists themselves to get the job done? Given the inherent provincialism of most science in the United States, is there not a prima facia case for government intervention in this instance of "market failure"?

One comment was repeatedly made by applied scientists in some fields: "We are the world leaders; why should we send our people out into the world?" It should be a cause for sober reflection that in areas where scientists in other nations are the world leaders they still keep their scouts on the trail.

A notable general characteristic of natural and physical scientists who go abroad for extended periods is that they tend to go for rather narrow purposes. In contrast to social scientists and humanists, whose continuing attraction may be "the people" or "the culture," the natural and physical scientist is likely to be oriented toward a particular person, problem, or instrument. This difference needs to be kept in mind by any program of support that encompasses all the disciplines together. If it is not, criteria for assistance that encompass one part of the scholarly community will exclude another.

Pursuit of personal goals

Some of our conversation partners in this study liked to make a clean distinction between professional and personal reasons for gaining international experience, implying, of course, a relatively frivolous cast to the latter set. We became increasingly convinced that such a distinction was seldom meaningful, because motives were not often clear, and results of actions undertaken for one purpose turned out to respond to another. For example, we spoke with one productive computer scientist who took a sabbatical leave from his university to work with an Israeli colleague at the Technion, a specialist in logic programming. He found that this visit not only transformed his academic research agenda, but at the same time served as an important family religious and cultural experience. It is useful to include here, then, one category of U.S. faculty who venture abroad for a congeries of objectives as broad as human nature. We exclude from this list the scientists, described above, who venture overseas periodically to reinvigorate their intellectual machinery. But we do include the academics who face boredom, discouragement, disillusionment, or simply the midlife crisis that is not associated exclusively with academe. Such scholars' batteries are well-charged, but there are other things wrong in their lives. For some such persons the medicine of foreign exposure does not achieve a cure of the particular ailment, but for many it does. For substantial numbers of U.S. academics the tonic of different intellectual outlook, cultural environment, and short-term personal and professional challenges has a long-lasting effect on teaching, research, and tolerance for a local community. These benefits are probed in more detail below. But it seems that they are sufficiently well perceived by faculty to generate a steady clientele for overseas activities.

We heard many terms, flattering and pejorative, used to de-scribe those who typically seek international experience when there is no evident professional benefit, not even the vague notion of intellectual rebirth: romantics, adventure-seekers, escapists, visionaries, and missionaries. They are perceived, at least, as aiming primarily in their travels at large philosophical objectives like global understanding or better international relations. Some observers thought they could detect waves of enthusiasm in this category reflecting political conditions, the presence or absence on campuses of groups like veterans of the armed forces or the Peace Corps and of study abroad alumni, and overall shifts in fashions in the academic world. Typically those in this category who had foreign experience in their careers had fewest terrors about going abroad again. They were sensitized already to the therapy that a foreign experience could entail.

Scholars who just say "No"

The characteristics of scholars who seek an international experi-ence are illuminated well by the contrast of those who do not. In our conversations those who had by choice not spent, or even considered spending, significant time overseas seemed to fall roughly into four groups. Each group has representatives from virtually all disciplines.

1. Know-it-alls

A position we heard expressed occasionally, more often in some fields than in others, and especially in the laboratory sciences, is

that all the good work is carried out in the United States. In part
this is explained as being a result of better instrumentation and
critical masses of scholars. But in addition, we were told, foreign
educational systems are derivative, teach mainly rote learning,
and stifle creativity. To the extent that other countries make contributions, it is likely to be the result merely of training in the
United States, emulating Americans, or collaboration with Americans. We were reminded often that the United States has received most Nobel Prizes by far. Those foreign contributions that
are deserving of attention by Americans, it was pointed out, appear in due course in the English-language journals, and there is
no reason to visit the countries of origin. Occasional long-range
collaborations with foreign scientists – and international conferences, of course – are appropriate offshore activities, but even
these are low on any responsible priority list and are legitimately
suspect of being "not serious."

Because after hearing this account of the significance of foreign laboratory science several times we were still unsure we had
heard it correctly, we repeated it to others in this stark form of
near caricature. When we did so we drew murmurs of assent
more often than qualifications or correction. There are two ways
to interpret this reaction. First, the scientists may be right, and
their unwillingness to attend to the rest of the world represents
the best use of scarce human resources. The second interpretation is that these scientists are like Napoleon before the Battle of
Waterloo, blinded by past success and unprepared for a grievous
fall. After one distinguished chemist told us that Japanese
chemistry was simply unworthy of serious attention by Americans, we remarked that this comment sounded a little like General Motors discussing Japanese automobiles in the 1960s. He re-
plied that that was an hysterical comment unworthy of serious
response and unwelcome from scholarly interviewers. ("You are
the worst interviewers I've ever met," he stated, apparently upset
that we sought to probe his skeptical views of foreign science.)

We came away from our many discussions with pure scientists
genuinely uncertain of which interpretation was most plausible.
We suspect that in some fields, at least, the first interpretation is

correct for the moment, but in others the second is creeping up fast. Should overseas workers in parts of pure science follow those in applied science and engineering and leapfrog over the present leaders in the United States, the U.S. scientific community is unprepared to respond. It behooves the scientific community to examine this possibility and take steps where necessary, including the development of richer international linkages.

When we got know-it-all scientists tightly wound-up on a campus, we were sometimes entertained by a conflict with their embarrassed and skeptical colleagues in other areas. On one occasion a nonscientist (a philosopher) turned on those know-it-alls and exploded, "You are nothing but windowless monads." (Definition: *Monad,* a spiritual being that is impenetrable.)

2. Lab-bound scientists

Many scientists in the United States, particularly senior and respected ones, even if alert to the benefits of close international contacts, are simply too overburdened with responsibilities to spend substantial periods abroad. Big science especially is a team effort, and the quarterback – or even a left guard – cannot simply walk away for a season. They have their research groups of junior faculty, postdoctoral fellows, and graduate students to attend. Above all, the team requires frequent refunding. There are requests for proposals (r.f.p.'s) to answer, reports to write, and funding agencies to soothe. But in addition there are research programs to sustain, personal conflicts to constrain, collaborations to retain, papers to complete, and voracious neighbors to fend off. "If I left for a year or even a semester," one group leader told us, "those guys would have my lab space." Some institutions were large enough for groups to have effective deputy leaders or other personnel willing to fill in, in a pinch, but these were the exception. One scientist put it this way. "When you're gone, you're gone – out of the loop. If you're absent for six months, it takes you two years to recover."

Overseas, moreover, the leader of a U.S. research team cannot expect simply to fit into someone else's team and thereby sustain his scholarly momentum. For such a person, overseas time is dead time, and on the treadmill of scholarly competition this is usually too high a price to pay. A chemist estimated for us that because of the high "opportunity cost," no more than one in twenty-five of his senior colleagues had been overseas for extended periods in the previous five years. He ventured that in his department a direct matchup with a distinguished foreign counterpart would be an acceptable reason for a period away; at the other extreme, teaching overseas would be seen simply as a waste of time.

If more intimate contact with the worldwide scholarly community than can be gained from brief meetings and conferences becomes necessary for scientific progress in the future, then those institutional structures that keep distinguished scientists tightly lab-bound must be reexamined and adjusted.

We were not able to discover anything like a complete consensus among laboratory scientists (chemists, biologists, and so on) about the professional benefit of an extended period overseas, even if problems on the home front were eliminated. The majority of those with whom we spoke thought their time was better spent in the lab at home, in any case. But a significant minority argued otherwise. One biochemist who has spent considerable time abroad said simply "The experience broadens you, and then you do better science. Techniques you learn at home; breadth you get abroad."

3. Methodologically sophisticated social scientists

Several of the social sciences have experienced a reaction in the twentieth century to institution-specific or nation-specific research. Instead of a focus on particularities and institutions, they have engaged in a search for universal regularities and generalizations. They seek to model human interactions through assumptions about rational actors and theories of rational choice. Data are needed to test and perfect such theories, but so long as human beings are perceived as fundamentally identical, American or computerized data-sets from other nations will do equally well.

There is certainly no need to ransack the world for seemingly irrelevant facts. Just as gravity in Chicago is identical to gravity in Kathmandu, so, it is implied, is voting behavior or consumer response to price. Indeed, to make a case that a deep and extended study of Nepal is necessary to appreciate Nepalese social behavior would be for some modern social scientists virtually to question the true fundamental *scientific* nature of the social sciences. To go abroad is to appear old-fashioned.

Accordingly we heard among the social sciences levels of enthusiasm for extended field trips abroad roughly inverse to their self-image of rigor, with the greatest skepticism expressed by "methodological mullahs" for whom theoretical modeling and quantifiable data (obtainable by mail from national statistical offices) and its analysis are the be-all and end-all of their professions. The typical "tough" social scientists, led by the economists, tended to agree with many of the biological and chemical scientists that practically all important science is now being carried out in the United States and will be so into the future. In addition, there is little need to go abroad to explore variety of data. Ergo, better stay home, and better examine (and consider penalizing) one's colleagues who do go for signs of bad judgment and moral weakness.

4. Some recent immigrants

As in the interviews for our earlier project on student programs abroad, we found fresh immigrants to the United States often sharply divided on the value of an overseas experience. Some do pine for, or at least take pride in, their old homelands and urge Americans to visit; they are often also enthusiastic advocates of the comparative method and advise Americans to venture elsewhere overseas. But other immigrants feel bitter about and disillusioned with the homeland that had not done more for them; they made a major psychological as well as geographical shift when they moved to the United States, and they can see neither much of value any longer in their former home nor much lacking in their adopted one, the United States. In particular, European scholars who have come recently to the United States because of poor employment prospects at home told us that the Old Country was really finished this time, that it was only sentimental nonsense that led Americans to consider leaving, even briefly, the land of opportunity. The United States, one told us, was the only source of true creativity today, and time spent elsewhere was time wasted. Another said, "This country is full of foreigners. Why should you go abroad to see more?"

5. The timid and the meek

For reasons enumerated in the next chapter, it must be admitted that an overseas academic experience can be arduous. Everything from health and finances to reputation and career may suffer. We and others conclude that in many cases the benefits still very significantly outweigh the costs, but the costs make the gamble a real one. Accordingly, those members of the scholarly community who are highly risk averse are simply not likely to seek such an opportunity at the start of the 1990s. If the nation wishes to change this situation, efforts will have to be made to reduce these risks.

6. Domestically oriented applied disciplines

Certain forms of professional education in the United States remain substantially without an international dimension. The reasons are not always clear. The greatest paradox is with study of the law. In our conversations we found surprisingly little enthusiasm among law school leaders for an internationalization of the curriculum or faculty research agenda. The exceptions we met were a few law school faculty expressly dedicated to comparative law – the study of Japanese, Chinese, Soviet, and other non-U.S. legal systems – and to international law. In contrast to business administration, divinity, and engineering, where the introduction of an international dimension is much discussed and the subject of considerable experimentation, in law the strong consensus among faculty is that the legitimate action lies at home, where the domestic courts can be watched in action and first-rate local libraries are at hand. There seems no inherent reason why there should be this distinction between law and the other applied fields; after all, lawyers can anticipate as many non-U.S. clients as can business people or engineers. In addition, lawyers have traditional responsibilities of political leadership for which international experience should be highly relevant. But many legal scholars do not seem to see it that way. One explanation we heard for this lack of interest is the lawyers' tendency to be a self-selected group of tough-minded antitheorists who delight in the particularities that arise on the home turf. One seemingly paradoxical result of the institutional discouragement of systematic internationalization of legal education and research is that individual legal scholars who do not accept this doctrine are among the most attractive applicants for individual overseas experiences. We have been informed of a movement among some professors of international law to internationalize law school curricula, but there was no evidence of this movement at the schools we visited.

One of the most provocative explanations we heard of the parochialism of U.S. law schools came from one of the relatively few professors of comparative law we encountered. He argued that legal studies in the United States have grown up in a manner closer to the study of religion than to an analytical social science. Just like the religious faithful, U.S. legal scholars stress particularity and look for truth at home. They don't go beyond their intellectual borders, except for brief visits, and certainly don't expect to learn from the priest of a rival sect. The critical legal studies movement that has sprung up at Harvard and elsewhere, designed, in part, to demonstrate the relativity of legal principles according to time and place, has met with exceptional hostility because it is like telling the converted of one religion that theirs is no better than another's, just different. At any rate, because the critical legal studies position usually carries considerable ideological baggage of its own, this professor argued that foreign study and experience are a better means of demonstrating the relativity of legal systems. A justification like this may be required to start a movement for internationalizing law schools comparable in any way to the development in business schools.

At one institution we visited, an exchange program in law had been established with government funding (Fund for the Improvement of Post-Secondary Education, or FIPSE). But we were advised the program would probably end with the end of funding. It was judged successful by most observers, but it was not perceived to advance institutional objectives sufficiently well to have a claim on internal resources.

We encountered a few clinical medical faculty with an interest in our subject, but they painted a rather consistently gloomy picture of their profession. They report that many physicians come to their calling with a strong sense of service, and this is translated easily into willingness to serve for periods in poor countries overseas. If physicians are concerned with public health, of course, they also see the world as their natural laboratory. But the system does not allow them to go abroad easily. The medical treadmill runs even faster than the scientific one. Like other parts of the sciences, the responsibility of senior faculty for a substantial number of dependent personnel, whether of a research or clinical kind, seems the biggest impediment. If more grant proposals are not constantly written, or patients seen, who will pay the technicians, the post-docs, the secretaries? Several of the medical faculty with whom we talked thought that they were likely to benefit as much as any in the sciences from a period abroad, but the arrangements would have to be for short, intensive stays. They could perceive the personal rewards but had to face the fact that with skeptical colleagues and innumerable dependents, the time costs had to be kept to a minimum.

3

Individual costs and benefits

This chapter and the next two are closely interrelated and even overlap to some degree. In this chapter we discuss the subjective elements that go into personal calculations in reaching a decision about going abroad. Chapter 4 reports campus attitudes to this decision, and Chapter 5 examines in detail the obstacles of various kinds that stand in the way of U.S. scholars going overseas. Although in fact the decision to go abroad rests on a complex calculation, it seems useful to sort out and reflect upon the components.

The considerations in the decision making may be divided into four categories: (1) personal costs, (2) personal benefits, (3) professional costs, and (4) professional benefits. Most of these have evolved significantly in recent years.

Personal costs

In many cases it is impossible to distinguish the real personal costs of an international experience from an individual's perceptions of these costs. Since both reality and perception affect decisions, both are important. The revolutionary advances in communications in recent years have had dramatic impact on perceptions. Just as vivid television reporting contributed, for example, to the termination of the Vietnam war, so the intimacy of telecommunications has influenced the understanding of costs and benefits of an international experience. This is true especially of personal costs.

1. Health and safety

We found a high level of concern among many faculty about potential health problems, not only for themselves, but for their families. Those having such concerns ranged from the Latin Americanist who wondered how many more bouts of gastrointestinal distress he could endure to the Asianist worried about malaria and the Africanist who wondered if he should carry quantities of his own blood to avoid AIDS-infected transfusions.

Personal safety was perceived as a more complex issue. Terrorism, coups d'état, and substantial animosity toward U.S. citizens were often cited as real hazards to be taken into account. The general decline of law and order was thought to be an omnipresent condition in some countries and when encountered was a terrifying experience. We were often regaled with stories of confinement to quarters while anarchy prevailed outdoors. One veteran of numerous periods abroad claimed he had been through five coups; in one of them the cabinet minister with whom he was working was jailed, and they simply transferred their conversations to prison! Some scholars said that because of political instability in Third World countries, they could no longer think of bringing their families. Yet leaving the family at home did not solve the problem because the widespread publicity given to the instability caused both the scholar and the family continuing anguish. Moreover, in the minds of relatively unsophisticated friends and family members, an evening news report of street violence in Buenos Aires or a drug war in Colombia, say, suggested that all of Latin America was in flames. More than one faculty member was reluctant to leave his wife and children to cope with the resultant anxiety over an extended period.

Although it is easy to make light of health and safety problems (indeed, the vast majority of scholars overseas emerge unscathed from the experience), we did hear of deaths and disabilities from tropical diseases, and we met an anthropologist who had been "detained" by the Nicaraguan contras. Perhaps most moving of all, as noted in the Introduction, during our visit there, the trees at Colorado State University were draped with yellow ribbons for Thomas Sutherland, a faculty member kidnapped while on leave at the American University of Beirut. In sum, the perception and reality of the threat of bodily harm abroad is a deterrent to some faculty; certainly it is a more credible deterrent than it was in the early days of academic travel immediately after World War II.

2. Finances

Virtually everyone with whom we spoke told of financial loss as a consequence of gaining international experience. Some spent savings; others took second mortgages on their homes. All came away with reduced net income. The reasons for the loss relate both to costs and to revenues. Invariably, unanticipated costs are encountered owing to high start-up and maintenance expenses, exacerbated by rapid inflation in many countries. But in addition, some expenses continue at home ("Somebody has to pay the mortgage") even as new ones pop up abroad. In some cases residence abroad for extended periods brings tax advantages, but for most this appears not to be an important compensating advantage.

On the revenue side few sabbatical leaves or research fellowships provide compensation equivalent to what would be received if one stayed home. Income forgone from consulting and other extramural activities adds to the revenue loss, differing in amount across academic fields. One faculty member abroad even lost a substantial income from moonlighting at home as a soccer referee! Fluctuating exchange rates contribute to the uncertainty and heartburn experienced by many faculty during a sojourn. A few, such as those visiting Brazil in recent years, reported net gains from exchange-rate fluctuations; most, however, told of serious losses.

An especially irksome revenue loss to persons serving abroad comes from the failure of home institutions to make significant merit pay increases during the absence. This custom reflects the prevailing judgment of many college and university administrators that whatever is going on "over there" is not meritorious. The loss of a step in the salary ladder is especially costly over the long term because its effects persist to the end of a career.

The clear impression we gained is that in the academic community the widespread perception is that, with the exception of foreign assistance employment under contract from public or private agencies, overseas experience involves significant personal financial loss. The greatest loss occurs in the conduct of research. There, dependence is upon fellowships or sabbatical pay, which are almost invariably below take-home levels in the United States. Somewhat less loss occurs in overseas teaching, either through exchange arrangements or in the leadership of study abroad programs. Rates of return to overseas teaching tend to come closer to market levels. This perception is accompanied by widespread bitterness about the implication of this situation, that individuals have to pay much of the cost of overseas research and teaching that should be seen as a real public benefit. The major policy question embedded in this situation is whether substantial numbers and kinds of faculty are really discouraged from going abroad by the true or perceived financial loss they will incur. Our strong impression is that financial pressures do indeed effectively discourage many faculty from spending extensive periods abroad.

3. Family complications

The changing character of the American family has created a host of new problems for the would-be academic traveler. Most important is the diffusion of decision-making authority within the family and the prevalence of two careers. As one person put it, "Twenty years ago when you got a Fulbright you went home and said, 'Start packing, dear.' If you tried that now, you might be told, 'Go climb a tree. I've got my clients to worry about.'" Even if the spouse agrees to go, there are the two incomes to make up somehow. And satisfying activities for both partners need to be arranged during the time abroad. Job discrimination, loss of merit pay increases, and other costs may be far greater for the employed spouse than for the academic on leave, and in extreme cases the spouse may even return to no job at all. Many families meet such challenges in various ways, and they do go abroad. But their special problems need to be recognized and, if possible, addressed.

Schooling for the children is one of the most pressing family problems when a period overseas is contemplated. Many observers claim that over the past several decades the primary and secondary school systems abroad have degenerated seriously, especially in countries of the Third World, to the point that school-age children simply cannot be brought along on extended visits. Since boarding schools are not in the culture of most U.S. academics and are too expensive to boot, educational responsibilities effectively proscribe activity for extended periods overseas while children are in school. Several faculty said that they were prepared, reluctantly, to sacrifice a very young child's formal education for a year or so abroad, but during the crucial college preparatory years (grades eight to twelve) uninterrupted U.S. residence was essential. It seems therefore that the best time for an overseas experience is early in an academic career, before children, or late in the career, when the children have left the home. The dilemma, of course, is that the middle years are often the most productive intellectually, the period in which faculty gain the most from an experience abroad.

When combined with the probationary period for tenure (discussed below), the constraint imposed by children's education suggests that many scholars may be seriously limited in accepting overseas assignments in the years between dissertation writing and advanced middle age when children are in college, a time when the adventurous ardor has cooled.

A good many, but certainly not all, of the family costs of an international experience are rooted in the lifestyle that has emerged for faculty in recent years both because they are better paid and because there are often two incomes. As one faculty member put it, "My wife, I, and each of the two kids has a car. If we go away, the payments keep coming, and they want cars where we're going. Who's going to pay for that?" Another faculty member observed that he could put up with the deprivation in creature comforts overseas, but his family wouldn't. We were told of several divorces that had been precipitated, or at least accelerated by the decline in life-style abroad and the strain of overseas service.

For many faculty the personal costs are combined in complex, interactive ways. One horror story illustrates the problem. We heard from a sociologist who, after much soul searching, took a substantial salary cut to accept a research award in Southeast Asia. When he got to his site, he found that his research materials were unexpectedly unavailable and his time was substantially wasted. When he returned home to a disgruntled family, he discovered his colleagues had punished him with an extra teaching load. There was no mistaking the cost-benefit ratio in this case.

Professional costs

The professional costs incurred from a departure overseas vary widely among individuals, institutions, and disciplines. In the most accommodating of colleges and universities and the most sympathetic of disciplines, penalties are likely to be minimal or nonexistent. Indeed, staying at home in these circumstances even has its perils. At the other end of the spectrum the costs in some fields and some places may be severe, up to and including failure to receive promotion and tenure. We heard such a range and variety of professional attitudes toward foreign travel that we can practicably sketch out only some of these here and urge faculty to ascertain the specific costs pertaining to their own circumstances.

1. Promotion and tenure

Among those who typically venture abroad we often found that the faculty in area studies and international disciplines most easily make good use of their time, by professional standards, manifested mainly in publications. As a rule, they receive a push upward on the academic ladder from their colleagues as a result. Although primary allegiance may be to an area studies program, foreign activities are perceived as legitimate within various disciplines.

Extensive travel is perfectly respectable, for example, for a Soviet economist, an Italian historian, or a sociologist specializing in Latin America. Indeed, even to a strict disciplinarian, reluctance to travel in an area study demonstrates lack of commitment. So long as the time abroad for the internationalist yields the nominal number of scholarly publications, the effort is widely viewed as legitimate and worthwhile within the discipline in which tenure is awarded. The same is true for scientists who pursue fieldwork, collaboration, and instrumentation in other countries. All others face lowered estimation by colleagues. Since international travel connotes both wealth and dissipation to many Americans, any overseas experience suggests the danger of incipient if not actual moral decay. As we have described above, this is true especially in those disciplines and subdisciplines whose practitioners typically stay home. This prejudice is widely distributed throughout academe, and young faculty members should fear its presence especially on college or university-wide advisory committees on promotion and tenure. Even in several institutions that have a strong commitment to development assistance we were told of committees with members outside the development fields penalizing those within for their international involvement.

The modern U.S. college and university is usually highly disaggregated, so subcommunities may develop their own standards and values. But the full community comes together on questions of professional advancement, and this is where the junior internationalist may suffer the prejudice of a provincial colleague and cannot be protected even by sympathetic seniors or institutional administrators.

2. Other professional detriments

Even if overseas service does not lead directly to constrained academic advancement, it can have other serious deleterious professional effects. It can interrupt a series of grants from a funding agency, cause a hiatus in publications and presentations at professional meetings, lose graduate students, and lead to defeats in the scramble for space. One scholar described the process as "losing the thread that takes you a year or so to find again." A scientist explained that "the downtime is so great, a period abroad is a high-stakes roll." A social scientist reported that typically the catch-up time required after return from a trip abroad stood in the way of the timely writing up of research. She said she still had depressing boxes of research notes looking down at her from her office shelves, marked "1981 trip," "1984 trip," "1986 trip." She questioned whether her findings would ever see the published light of day. The seriousness of the disjuncture caused by a time abroad depends, of course, on the rules and regulations of the institution. Nevertheless we came away convinced that for many capable, well-intentioned researchers it is difficult to translate experience abroad into publishable output because upon return, in addition to needing readjustment to their local scholarly climate, they are inundated with academic responsibilities that arise from their absence.

3. Attitudes of colleagues

The views of academic associates determine, in part, whether career advancement is affected positively or negatively by activity abroad. They also affect life in myriad other ways. In general, we found that those who do not travel, for whatever reason, do not harbor much love for those who do. We heard the typical attitude of the nontraveler described as "vibrating somewhere between admiration, envy, and contempt." The suspicion of nontraveling colleagues is that the time abroad is all "fun and games." As one victim of ill feelings told us, "They can't believe that anything you enjoy that much is serious." A young scholar in particular must think carefully about the real costs of incurring the effects of such attitudes. Evidently a frequent "punishment" for those returning from overseas is an extra teaching and committee load. "You've been on vacation, you must be ready for it."

Professional benefits

Some professional benefits of foreign experience are obvious. Others are less so. In the most general sense a foreign experience may be viewed as a highly valuable part of the lifelong learning process through which a scholar passes. As one person put it, "Education is learning how to learn, and this requires a worldwide compass." But at a level of greater particularity there are more specific benefits that can be placed in several narrower categories.

1. Data and ideas

The stimulus for much scholarly travel overseas is the need to gather materials, whether in the field or in the library, important for research. A second objective is to share ideas with foreign colleagues and learn about and from them. Contacts are made and names matched with faces. A third objective is to try out methodologies, modes of thought, and hypotheses in environments, both physical and social, very different from those for which they were originally designed. As one veteran put it, "You can talk, look, ask stupid questions, and burn your fingers. There is no other way of getting this interaction. If you stayed home, you couldn't quiz a published article." An economist brings his market models to the Soviet Union. An obstetrician visits a society dominated by nurse midwifery.

An unusual but not unheard-of professional benefit of time abroad is to discover an entirely new subdiscipline unknown in the home country. For example, one philosopher told us about being introduced overseas to the philosophy of technology, to which he now devotes all his effort. Even in disciplines where it is widely acknowledged that the United States is in the vanguard, pockets of exceptional strength may be discovered abroad. Gerontologists learn in China, and civil rights scholars report debts to European experiences. A civil engineer objected vigorously to what he called "academic voyeurism," meaning scholars who dashed into a country expecting short-term gain. He believed fervently in the utility of the growing practice of sustained collaborative relationships abroad and illustrated the point with reference to the following Turkish proverb: "If just looking made you a master, all dogs would be butchers."

The likelihood of finding unique intellectual resources overseas is explained in part by the variety of the human race. The wider the search, the greater the probability of success. In the modern world access to both data and ideas requires increasingly sophisticated interactions. Cooperative endeavors of various kinds are becoming a preferred mode of accomplishing this end. Happily, improvements in transportation and communications make collaboration more and more practical. Several scientists with whom we spoke placed collaboration at the head of all benefits gained from foreign travel. We encountered an astonishing number and variety of collaborations already in place: Among many others, a polymer chemist has a career-long relationship with a Soviet theorist; a voice teacher brings his students each summer to a European music festival; an engineering professor teaches his speciality in English to Arab students at the Budapest Institute of Technology; a historian of the holocaust has become part of the community engaged on this subject in Europe and Israel.

2. Teaching improvement

Enough scholars testified to improvement in their teaching as a result of experience overseas for us to conclude that some generalized phenomenon must exist. The improvement seems to have several roots. In the humanities, the social sciences, the professions, and the applied natural sciences time overseas provides a wealth of institutional material, anecdote, and comparative perspective. As one person put it, no amount of "book learning" can substitute beyond a certain point for foreign experience. A teacher of Spanish language and culture, who studied in graduate school in Mexico, told us of her first revelatory visit to Madrid. For years she had been telling her students of the universal public celebration of the downfall of the Franco regime; yet on her first evening she heard nothing but complaints from her landlord and his friends about how things had gone downhill since Franco; the trains didn't run on time anymore, for example. On her first day she went to visit a madonna about which she had lectured for years from a slide displayed at life size on her classroom wall; she discovered to her astonishment that it was only twelve inches tall.

Within twenty-four hours she was completely disoriented, she said, but by the end of her visit she was certain that she was far better informed and would be a vastly improved teacher upon her return.

More generally, we were told repeatedly, the experience abroad seems to generate a sympathy toward students – both American and foreign – and their problems, which take on a new meaning upon the return home. One person even suggested that prospective teachers of large numbers of foreign students in any field should be required beforehand to spend an extended period abroad. Only in this way could they gain the necessary degree of sensitivity and experience. There is near-unanimity that faculty return from abroad better positioned to be effective counselors to students of all backgrounds and perspectives.

Foreign experience improves teaching in the generalized fashion just described, but it is also beneficial when the subject matter is highly specialized, for example, area studies or a well-focused international or comparative subdiscipline. In theory teachers in such fields are expected to refresh their competence by conducting research and fieldwork, and immersing themselves in the current advanced literature. In practice, we all know, these modes of refreshment end for many scholars soon after leaving graduate school or at least long before the end of a teaching career. One liberal arts college acknowledged openly that their area studies specialists would in most cases "never play in the big leagues" or compete successfully for the major fellowships that would bring them back to "the field." This college quite self-consciously used the direction of study abroad programs to move its area studies faculty back to their areas at regular intervals. It found this faculty refreshment function a significant side benefit of operating overseas study programs for undergraduates.

3. The inevitability of unpredictable consequences

Perhaps the most frequent comment we heard about an overseas experience was that the results are almost never fully anticipated. For example, we listened to extensive testimony about fundamental changes of research path that took place abroad but had never been contemplated. A Renaissance art historian becomes a specialist on Italian culture; a mathematician shifts to pedagogy appropriate for the Third World; a clinical psychologist becomes a specialist on drug addiction in several societies; an experimental psychologist learns about different comparative behavior patterns; an area studies specialist switches to global refugee studies; a sociologist, to demography. Several persons reported that with respect to shifts in career direction a foreign experience provided both push and legitimation. Because of the almost mystical character of the transformation in some faculty when they go abroad we heard numerous metaphors used to explain the process. One talked of "reloading." Another spoke of gaming: "You shuffle the deck and place the cards in new formations." Still another referred to change in the scholar's usual life pattern: "You dump the file drawers on the ground and pick them up in different combinations." A historian said: "The stimulus to intellectual creativity is like that of the peripatetic Medieval schoolmen." A scientist observed: "Exposure to archaeology may retard burnout in a mathematician, but you can't be sure it will or say why."

One unexpected result reported by several persons grows out of the special conditions of the small colleges from which they come. Where departments are not large enough to appoint several persons in any one subdiscipline, it is often difficult for a young person to establish a "professional focus" for teaching and research. Although this process may occur for such a person during a postdoctoral period at a major U.S. research center, there is ample testimony that it also happens abroad. In addition to career shifts, we heard about cooperative relationships between laboratories that lasted decades and flows of graduate students back to the home campus that never seemed to dry up. On several occasions we heard of eye-opening experiences with scholarly cultures different from the American, demonstrating that much could be accomplished even in academic environments that lack the workaholism and rush to publication that are our hallmark. Serendipity, of course, operates vigorously on the American scene as well as overseas. But it must be present in greater intensity and variety when faculty go abroad.

In contrast to many administrators who picture foreign experience as a time in the fleshpots, with innumerable destructive blandishments to which any weak-willed faculty member is likely to succumb, one enlightened administrator suggested that the institutional benefits of serendipity – bridges built, inertia combated, old icons broken – amply justified institutional support and encouragement. His worry was not that faculty were likely to be lured away too often, but rather that the personal attractions were not enough to stimulate a desirable level of travel. External stimuli were obviously essential. Comparing scholarly travel to taking bad-tasting medicine, he saw the problem as getting the "patient" to swallow a sufficient dose.

4. Luster to the résumé

The conditions under which a faculty member travels abroad determine the increment added thereby to professional prestige. Guggenheim or National Endowment for the Humanities senior fellowships and the like connote quality. The same cannot be said unequivocally for other means. Faculty, and especially those at prominent institutions, have a sensitive nose for market conditions. They have a strong sense now that Fulbright grants are not sufficiently lucrative to attract only first-rate people. Therefore, to have had one seems not to be singular evidence of distinguished accomplishment. Only at less prominent institutions did we find the luster of the Fulbright still uniformly bright. Service abroad on an AID contract seems often to dull professional luster because it is assumed that the scholar had no time to conduct research and thereby accumulate publications, the scholar's legal tender.

Personal benefits

The personal benefits from a foreign experience are in some respects rooted in the same causes that generate costs. They may however be less tangible, even though no less real.

1. Self-understanding

Almost all we interviewed told us that they learned much about themselves and their society when lifted out of their familiar environment and regimen. One scientist told us that he came to appreciate his own language only when he had to struggle with another. Usually this personal revelation is converted into changes in personal and professional style. A frequent comment was that immersion in another culture, especially one in the Third World, raises one's level of sensitivity, tolerance, and empathy for the problems of others. Another comment was that the experience teaches you more about yourself and your country than about others. A political scientist, exhausted after an extended tour in China, claimed that from that distant vantage point he had learned more about our own norms and values – who we are – than he had about the Chinese. One faculty member described a Fulbright year as "the most exciting and disrupting" in his career. He urged that foreign experience be gained early, while a person is more flexible and able to benefit from the impact and the culture shock.

2. Family participation

The challenges and hurdles that can create deep tensions in the U.S. family overseas can also strengthen the family bonds. Academic life in the United States, especially at large urban universities, tends to isolate the faculty member from spouse and children. This seldom happens abroad. The entire family must work together to meet and resolve the problems and crises that arise for all members. Team spirit is simply essential for survival. Matching the stories of difficulties and "catastrophes" (the term used by one faculty member whose family left him after the year abroad), we heard accounts of positive outcomes and triumphs in the face of significant obstacles. The mere fact of joint struggle with unfamiliar surroundings is perceived by some as valuable in itself. Others told how their children's futures, as well as their own, had been shaped for the better by the experience.

3. *A chance to serve*

Some argue that many academics choose their profession because of a sense of mission. They wish to share their knowledge
with those who want to learn, even if the financial rewards are
less than in other occupations. Like the number of clerics among
the professoriate in the nineteenth century, the number of Peace
Corps alumni today reflects the prominence of voluntarism in the
academic mentality. But there are remarkably few outlets for
voluntarism in the mainstream of academic life. Indeed, on U.S.
college campuses "service" is usually last in importance and prestige in the eyes of faculty peers and is thought of as reserved for
those who can no longer "cut the mustard" in research in their
own disciplines. Service overseas can be a highly rewarding opportunity that retains some respectability. Most obviously projects of development assistance agencies fall within this category,
as do Fulbrights in the Third World. But other exchanges, and
even some study abroad programs, contain the element of worthy
self-sacrifice that is associated with service. One specialist in
Women's Studies found that the most rewarding aspect of her time
abroad was the opportunity to share this distinctly American field
with others who are only beginning to develop an interest in it.

Those who pursue an international experience because of the
opportunity for service often select a teaching option over research or technical assistance. However, we met a distressingly
large number of these who expressed deep disillusionment over
and frustration with the experience because of the anarchic conditions of foreign colleges and universities. They felt they had
made the sacrifice without making much contribution. Their near-
ly universal recommendation was that, whenever possible, teaching be directed toward *foreign faculty,* rather than toward foreign
undergraduate or even graduate students. This ensures that the
talents of the visitor are well used and not simply thrown at the
student hordes. Unfortunately, too many faculty had experiences
similar to one who had taught undergraduates in Beijing, where
his hosts greeted him on arrival, pointed to the huge classes, and
said, "Hello, nice to meet you. We'll have a banquet before you
leave."

4. A wider horizon

One of the widely acknowledged benefits of study abroad for students at small liberal arts colleges is the chance to get away, to savor the world outside after feasting on the fruits of the small community. The same benefit seems to exist for faculty members. Even for those who rejoice in isolation there is often a need for contrast, and there is no greater opportunity for contrast than a period abroad. At one college a group of faculty from several disciplines agreed that although they enjoyed a strong sense of college community, campus life was healthier overall when faculty looked beyond their walls for "standing, prestige, credentials and validation." Colleagues gain perspective on each other by achieving distance. The dangers of introversion are overcome by occasional glances, at least, over the walls, and by visits. One of the particular benefits from foreign travel comes in gaining cultural humility. One observer, recalling Lyndon Johnson's oft-quoted observation, noted that "most Americans assume everyone else wants to become an American. It is a sobering discovery to find they don't."

On one college campus local camaraderie and sense of commitment make any off-campus activity seem positively disloyal. Sabbatical leaves go unused, and the dean says faculty have to be virtually kicked off campus. In this situation a foreign interlude offers special benefits, both to the individuals and the institution.

4

Campus attitudes

Faculty departures overseas occur within a climate of opinion that may affect the decision to go – and certainly will affect the traveler's reception on return. There are, of course, on any campus as varied a set of attitudes as the variety of characters who make up the academic community. Moreover, attitudes cannot easily be discerned from formal statements; rhetoric on this, as on many subjects, often departs widely from reality. Whenever possible on our travels, when exploring attitudes, we looked for evidence of action that confirmed the talk. For example, if a faculty body applauded international experience, we asked whether it also rewarded those who went abroad in the tenure and promotion process. When presidents or provosts testified to the importance of an international campus, did they also make the budget adjustments that were required to cause this to happen?

It did seem possible in some cases to pick up the ethos of an entire institution respecting the subject of our inquiry. For example, in one we encountered little but cynicism toward anything that occurred off its campus, let alone overseas. In this prestigious liberal arts college it was argued vehemently by the provost that the institution was essentially a "prep school for graduate school" with top-notch faculty and first-rate students. Any time spent by faculty away from the campus, except for specialized research trips, was fundamentally counterproductive to the basic mission of the institution. At the other extreme, at one major private university the expectation was clearly understood that everyone would and should go abroad at every opportunity, and colleagues were puzzled that anyone would not seek foreign travel. But by and large, in order to discover attitudes of an academic community, we found it necessary to separate the members into groups. Although we remain cautious about generalizing about these smaller aggregations, we have identified patterns that may at least be tested by others against conditions on their own campuses.

As we pressed for comment on foreign experience, we picked up a range of adjectives from those who traveled that reflected a kind of attitudinal spectrum. At one extreme some members of the campus community are "negative" and "opposed." Some faculty spoke of their entire institution as "obstructive" or an "obstacle" to gaining foreign experience. In the middle, the most populous category in the institutions we visited, were those perceived by various interviewees as "neutral," "passive," "reactive," and "agnostic." At the other extreme stood those who were totally "active," "enthusiastic," and "positive" about the acquisition of international experience. Some interviewees agreed to locate for us, somewhere on this spectrum, the weight of opinion on their own campus and then to assess whether that opinion had shifted markedly in recent years. Most pointed somewhere in the middle range, with perhaps a slight shift over time in a positive direction.

It is useful to examine the attitudes typically reflected by the familiar parts of an academic institution.

The central administration

Our sample of thirty-eight institutions may have been too small to illuminate fairly the condition of the leadership of U.S. higher education. Nevertheless we came away, surprisingly, with a prevailing sense of unease. So many presidential chairs were vacant on our arrival that we feared we might be a jinx. Among those chairs that were filled we found the incumbents frequently beleaguered in various ways and seldom able to reflect seriously on a subject seemingly as vague and long-range as the international experience of their faculty. In many places a financial crisis was impending or at hand, and that took the central administration's full attention. Indeed, it would be hard to exaggerate the sense of financial precariousness that prevails today in U.S. higher education, from state universities that are experiencing contractions imposed by state legistatures to liberal arts colleges that are facing potentially catastrophic enrollment declines. Like hanging, the prospect of financial instability or even bankruptcy wonderfully concentrates the minds of academic leaders – to the exclusion of all else. For example, at one Jesuit college that we hoped would exemplify a concern for international study in the tradition of the Roman Catholic Church we found that the senior administrator was paying single-minded attention to "the bottom line." This meant the enrollment and retention of fee-paying students and the attraction of overhead-paying research were the sole bases for policy. At a major research-oriented public university the provost exclaimed rather distractedly: "I don't know how I am going to sustain a first-class library or state-of-the-art science, and you come to talk to me about faculty abroad!" Behind comments like this, it was clear, lay the conviction within academic administrations that, with the exception of development assistance contracts, international research and teaching never bring in the overhead recovery experienced on domestic projects. In their terms, fellowships and personal consulting for faculty simply don't pay off. At best, they believe, internationalization may be a loss leader. But when you are hovering on the brink of insolvency, losses for any purpose are simply intolerable.

A compensating effect of financial stringency on a few campuses was support for faculty travel in those directions that for one reason or another were perceived as likely to yield some financial rewards to the institution, either in U.S. or foreign funding. It is currently fashionable for many to pin hopes for gold at the end of the rainbow mainly on Japan and the Pacific Rim, where, it is believed, generous donors may be willing to fund those who evince a serious interest in their region. In addition, faculty experience overseas was perceived by a few senior administrators, especially those in newer colleges and universities, as giving distinction to the institution, particularly when funded by prestigious fellowships, and this improved reputation was thought to have financial implications through the attraction of donors and good students.

If pressed, a president could sometimes dig out of a drawer a speech delivered at commencement some years ago or a mission statement prepared for an accrediting body, calling for a "global campus." But when we asked for specifics, the eyes would glaze and the talk would turn quickly to the short-sightedness and stinginess of the state legislature or to some other issue of current concern. With respect to one past presidential utterance, a disgruntled faculty member grumbled that his leader "does not put his resources where his rhetoric is." At one exceptional institution a new president did just that by announcing that if a faculty member could find a quarter of the cost of a worthwhile trip, he would find the rest.

We must not give the impression of a complete absence of senior academic leadership on the question of internationalization. There were significant exceptions. One college president spoke eloquently of his vision of liberal education as freeing students from the tyranny of habit, custom, and ethnocentricity. To achieve this, he was absolutely certain, the faculty must understand the world. In order to get faculty abroad, he proposed to depend very heavily on multicollege consortia that could do what one institution could not. In another institution the president deliberately adopted a plan of promoting faculty visits abroad as a means of recruiting foreign students. This was done to compensate for declining local student enrollments and to internationalize the staff at the same time.

We could discern international experience of faculty in only one central administration's strategic plan (when there was a plan!), and in that case the president had been fired two days before our arrival, so we were unable to talk with him about it.

On some campuses there is lodged somewhere within the administration responsibility for a process called faculty development. Although international experience might be recognized as a part of this process, we found little evidence that it was.

We asked presidents and provosts where the international experience of their faculty stood in their hierarchy of priorities. It was usually well behind the search for a new football coach or the construction of a parking garage. We were often told, in effect, "We will get on with that when we have more money," which is another way of saying it doesn't matter very much. This posture tended to support the oft-expressed view of the internationalist faculty that they are marginal people, slow to be given support and quick to be cut off when troubles appear. One shrewd observer suggested to us that one reason why senior administrators seldom referred to overseas experience of faculty, even while waxing eloquent on internationalization, was from an instinctive fear of how this experience would "play" with their public constituency (legislators, alumni, donors, the local press), which thought of foreign travel still as equivalent to attending the Folies Bergère. The suspicion may be strongest in rural areas. When we pressed one provost on his seeming lack of interest, he conceded that foreign experience might be important for "culture-bound" disciplines (the humanities and social sciences); for the rest, however, he found the issue trivial.

The faculty

Beyond those in area studies and departments or subdisciplines where overseas activities are widely accepted as essential to scholarly activity we detected a general skepticism among faculty members about giving special attention, encouragement, or even discussion to the subject of an international experience. As we probed, we were led to conclude that the explanation for this position lay perhaps both in the peculiar mores of American academe and in the course of American social development.

The practice in U.S. academic life of constructing a set of quite precise hurdles (the Scholastic Aptitude Tests, the lockstep doctorate, promotion through the ranks to distinguished chair) over which faculty members must jump to receive rewards conflicts directly with the rather vague and intangible talk of benefits derived from an international experience. We often heard faculty members express their support for such experiences so long as a colleague's "productivity" (that is, articles in respected journals) did not suffer. Although lip service might occasionally be given to objectives other than publication, the implication was clear that these should be gained by scholars "on their own time" and not at the expense of what really mattered, acceptance by conventional publications.

Most faculty, not surprisingly, were vigorously opposed to institutional planning that would increase their foreign exposure. Faculty are opposed to virtually all planning that might constrain their freedom. The more assertive, typified by an eloquent professor of English at a prestigious New England liberal arts college, told us repeatedly that the function of the ideal college or university administration was to implement the wishes of the faculty, and these wishes would certainly not include the identification of international experience as a communal goal. Travel should concern only the individual faculty members themselves in the privacy of their personal decision making.

It was striking that what one commentator referred to as "the psychology of anarchy" and another called the doctrine of laissez-faire seemed pervasive throughout academe. It was present as much, for example, in the intense, conservative, high-style liberal arts college as in the radical, 1960s-origin institution. The significance of this condition for our inquiry is that, on the one hand, it limits most kinds of planning that might stimulate faculty internationalization, and on the other hand, it does not provide for the protection of those faculty who contravene deep-rooted prejudices by spending extensive periods abroad.

The larger social *gestalt* and academic mores affect faculty attitudes, we conclude, in that many professors, like legislators and bureaucrats, still harbor the sense that foreign travel is really a luxury for the rich: a vacation, possibly a boondoggle, and unlikely to produce serious scholarly work. In its more charitable form the skeptic's attitude was typified by a colleague remarking to an international fellowship winner: "Oh, you dog. Congratulations on getting it and getting away with it. Save some for me." Even some who were not so cynical were still skeptical of the research payoff of foreign travel because of the numerous obsta-

cles (for example, limited access to good data, poorly run universities) that they knew scholars encountered overseas.

Another campus attitude rooted in the larger American culture
is a reflection of the myth of the melting pot. The United States,
this myth teaches, has created a great new nation out of bits of
decadent older ones. Assimilation is the essence of the American
spirit, and refreshment at the springs of origin may be seen as
tantamount to cultural treason.

One observer described the professoriate on his campus as
"the bastion of reaction," and on the subject of international travel we suspect this generalization may be of wide application. One
of the more depressing dimensions of this generalization is that it
seems to hold in many cases more with the younger than with the
older faculty, although, of course, the young were made narrow
and goal-oriented by their elders.

Lest one conclude that on a campus it does not matter to a
widely traveled anthropologist or civil engineer that a chemist or
microbiologist is deeply skeptical of their overseas activities, it
should be recalled, as we have already noted, that in academic
communities personnel and sometimes budgetary decisions are
made collectively by colleagues from many fields – moreover,
that chemist might become the dean!

Veterans of extended periods abroad on campuses inhospitable to travel confided to us some of their survival tactics. First of
all, they advised, never send home, even in jest, cards that say
"weather lovely, beach beautiful, eat your heart out." Take every
opportunity to demonstrate the academic purpose of your absence and the seriousness of your intent. Do everything possible
to prevent jealousy and ignorant prejudice from rising to the
surface.

One might expect that specialists in particular geographical
areas, and frequent travelers in general, would be uniformly enthusiastic advocates of all faculty travel, and indeed many are.
But we encountered two significant exceptions. First, some faculty who have devoted careers to acquiring foreign expertise feel
resentment at newcomers who would like now to jump in without
paying the price as it were. Sometimes these old hands are in the

front of the pack who deplore the aspirations of "dilettantes." The
second exception is persons who favor a division of labor respecting travel, from which they are the distinct beneficiaries. Their
view toward stay-at-home colleagues is "I'll do the travel; you
tend the home fires." Often this division has existed for many
years, with most in a department accepting the notion that there
are several cosmopolitan colleagues who will represent the institution abroad, almost like a foreign service. The notion that
international experience is valuable to everyone in the department is a distinct threat to the life-style of these cosmopolitans.
This form of self-serving elitism is usually camouflaged behind
some other argument, like the necessity of long experience in
foreign travel or great language fluency, but a little scraping away
of rhetoric quickly identifies the true motives. Naturally those
assigned to the home fires may easily become unhappy at the
arrangement.

The relatively rare condition under which all faculty are enthusiastic about foreign travel usually occurs where the experience is
widely and equally shared among active and self-confident colleagues. Then anyone's inconvenience at a colleague's absence is
soon compensated by his or her own departure.

Deans and department chairs

We found the middle management of most institutions attentive
above all to fashion and to funding. If other comparable schools
or departments are internationalizing, as is the perception, for
example, at many business schools and in some engineering departments, then deans and chairs are tuned in and turned on. If
their opposite numbers are not doing it, as is the case in law and
most basic sciences, then interest in minimal. This suggests the
importance of making change in the lead departments and schools
in the country and in the professional and disciplinary societies. If
one of these can be persuaded to change course, a herd of imita-
tors will likely follow.

Finances affect the interests of middle management directly
through the institutional arrangements governing the treatment of

a departed faculty member. If the salary savings from an absence are captured by some administrator up the line, then the dean or chair is left with all the jobs of the faculty member to do and with no one and little or no money wherewith to do them. If, on the other hand, the department or school is truly a "tub on its own bottom," with responsibility for its own revenues and expenditures, then the incentives are great to coax senior faculty away from the campus, cover them with less expensive staff, and pocket the difference for discretionary purposes.

The effects of the revolving door principle in American academic administration are especially evident at the middle level. We sense that most of the deans and chairs with whom we spoke perceived their appointments as so short term that they cannot easily get their minds around notions like long-term faculty development growing out of an international experience. They feel their job is well done if posts are filled, classes taught, committees staffed, and regulations not transgressed unreasonably. The horizon is short term and practical. As one dean asked us, "If international experience is an input, to what output about which I am now concerned does it contribute?" If the answer we gave was "published research," this was easily grasped; if it was "teaching" or "service," there was considerable skepticism; if it was anything else, there was simply disbelief. At several smaller and weaker institutions we heard suggestions that deans feared international travel by their most able faculty, as they did all departures from the campus, because this was likely to bring the travelers more attractive job opportunities.

The administrative revolving door does more than assure executive timidity; it also engenders uncertainty among faculty. One dean, chair, or president may encourage foreign travel, and the successor punish it.

Once more this picture of deans and chairs should not be seen as unremittingly gloomy. One sympathetic dean observed that faculty will do everything better if "something gets their creative juices flowing," and increased flow was his impression of what often happened abroad. Another dean spoke of international experience causing faculty to shift back into high gear after a sus-

tained loss of enthusiasm following their graduate education. But
these deans were very much the exception.

Faculty, especially younger ones, often expressed regret to us
that their deans failed to provide leadership in "the uphill battle
against provincialism." One young internationalist described
his dean as oscillating between passivity and mild interest. He
yearned for "coordination, cross-fertilization, and demonstration
of institutional commitment." Faculty in engineering and business schools, despite the avowed efforts of these units to internationalize, suspected that their deans were cooperating only with
suppressed kicks and screams. If off-campus work was necessary, the typical professional school dean, they insisted, far preferred that faculty work at and cement good relations with local
corporations.

Students

We were fascinated to discover in several places that students
seemed to be the instigating force in developing a high level of
campus international awareness, moving, in fact, well ahead of
the faculty and administration. Undoubtedly some of this student
interest in the world comes from genuine intellectual curiosity,
but much originates, we were assured by their faculty, from a
strong sense that sophisticated knowledge of world affairs will be
necessary for a good job in the twenty-first century, if not before.
Student pressure for internationalization was clearly evident in
several of the professional schools (reflected in demands expressed by high-quality applicants for admission), but it was also
present in liberal arts colleges, where students were unwilling to
put up with international studies perceived as unsatisfactory – or
with the nonexistence of such studies. At one predominantly
black college with a strong African Studies program enthusiasti-
cally supported, for domestic reasons, by the 1960s-trained faculty, we were told regretfully by one administrator that the students were insisting on an East Asian program because of its job
relevance: "Our students want opportunities in Japan and Korea,
where the economic action is, not in sub-Saharan Africa." Stu-

dents, of course, usually have limited direct impact upon anything as remote as a faculty member's decision to gain foreign experience, but they do vote with their feet, both when making choices among courses and departments and when picking those schools that demonstrate objectives and styles they find attractive.

External agents

Various forces outside the academic community have played decisive roles in affecting the international activities of faculty. Foreign assistance agencies and fellowship programs like Fulbright, discussed in Chapter 2, still play leading roles in facilitating foreign travel, especially at land-grant institutions. The large private foundations were especially active in earlier years in encouraging international studies across a broad front. Now they are much more selective and focused. The church in some places has a major part and in others a relatively minor one. Evidence at the Catholic institutions we visited did not suggest that that church today places unusually high emphasis on knowing the wider world. The Mormon Church, on the other hand, requires many of its members to serve abroad as missionaries, causing most faculty who share their faith to come equipped with fluency in a foreign language and an extended residency abroad, even if a rather unusual one. Most Mormon young men between the ages of eighteen and twenty-one take a two-year stint abroad to seek foreign converts. Although they are often isolated from much of the society in which they live, they learn a foreign language well and sometimes return with a keen interest in other cultures.

The business community, represented on the governing boards of most colleges and universities, generates a climate of opinion more often than pressing for particular actions or reforms. In general business people wish for internationalization of campuses in proportion to the extent that they themselves depend on foreign trade or investment. In doing so they reflect self-interest in seeking informed employees and consultants. In addition, as they themselves become more cosmopolitan and better traveled, they

conclude that it is remarkable for others not to be so broadly
informed. Business schools in particular have demonstrated that
funds can be raised from the business community to support the
internationalization of faculty.

The attitude of the business community toward campus inter-
nationalism is certainly not all positive. At one private university
charges of "globalism" (meaning neglect of U.S. interests and the
undermining of patriotism) in an international studies institute
brought down the ire of conservative business leaders and left the
entire academic community nervous and jittery when the subject
of internationalization was raised.

At some institutions we visited, especially on the West Coast,
the high school experiences of their matriculants necessitated
internationalizion. It was not possible, they found, to tell a high
school graduate with several years of instruction in Japanese language and culture that the college or university had neither advanced curricula nor sophisticated faculty to meet their needs. If
one institution could not respond positively to such demands,
students would go to another that did. In circumstances like this,
high school graduates with language training were reflecting the
values and wishes of the larger society as interpreted by local
school boards. In this way society guides higher education indi-
rectly.

At the other end of the educational experience alumni also
exert pressure for internationalization. At a distinguished engineering institution renowned for the technical skills of its graduates, a survey of alumni revealed deep dissatisfaction with the
lack of preparation that they had been provided for positions of
corporate leadership in the modern world. One alumnus reported
that when appointed head of a major oil company and required
suddenly to reorganize the firm's operations in Manila, he could
not find the Philippines on the map. Another was working in Chile
at the time of the Pinochet coup d'état and had never heard of
Allende. The results of this survey precipitated one of the most
imaginative efforts we encountered to internationalize a campus.
The academic leaders recognized that for engineers working
abroad an understanding of cartels and state-owned enterprises

or of the process of redemocratization may be as crucial to success as the techniques of Computer-Aided Design, Computer-Aided Manufacturing (CADCAM) or dam construction. This is discussed in more detail in Chapter 7.

One of the means whereby the views of the outside community about internationalization are communicated forcefully to a college and university is via an external visiting committee or board of visitors. We spent time at several institutions where, reportedly, these bodies had been effective instigators of change. It was striking that at land-grant universities boards of visitors and state legislators alike took particular pride in foreign assistance activities. There seemed little feeling that faculty should stay home and tend to their local knitting. The only exception was where assistance was provided directly to a competitor industry in a foreign country. There seems to be a distinction between pride in an institutional program with an international focus and envy of, and doubts about, individuals with international interests.

Considering the innate conservatism of faculty and the general lack of interest among college and university administrators in international experience, we came away from our discussions wondering whether, without external agents, U.S. higher education in the late 1980s was any more experienced internationally than it had been fifty years before. This is a sobering reflection in that all of these agents are ephemeral and even fickle.

5

Obstacles to international experience

For those who think a cosmopolitan scholarly community is important to the United States both in its task of passing on accumulated knowledge to young minds and in its responsibility to produce new knowledge, it may be useful to offer a recapitulation of the impediments that stand in the way of the continued and expanded flow of American scholars for extended periods overseas. These obstacles fall naturally into four categories reflecting, respectively, the nature of the financial support available, the institutional context of the home colleges and universities, hostility faced by would-be travelers from the larger culture of this country, and conditions they face in the countries where they go. Some readers, having read the discussion of these obstacles in Chapters 3 and 4, may wish to proceed directly to Chapter 6. However those who are concerned with policy change to remedy the condition may find this drawing together useful.

To list these obstacles is not to suggest that they can be easily overcome or eliminated. Indeed, the best strategy for many may simply be circumvention. But recognition of problems is the first step toward their solution, and this enumeration is presented in that spirit.

Finding the funding

The increasing importance attached to assistance contracts and study abroad directorships as a means to gain experience overseas reflects the shortage of funds for conventional research-oriented study tours. Not only are there very few programs that provide overseas awards, but like the Fulbrights, most have lost value relative to faculty salaries. There are virtually no research awards available today that will match the home institution's salary, let alone the real full cost of going abroad for a moderately senior faculty member. Even with partial sabbatical pay, faculty bent on research can avoid serious loss only by hustling around to put together an acceptable package from several sources. The effects of this requirement are several. First, it reduces the attractiveness and therefore the prestige of awards and of the whole practice of scholarly exchange. Second, it selects out and keeps at home a certain kind of scholar, one who either does not have the talent to scrape together the bits and pieces of a salary equivalent or is unwilling to make a significant financial sacrifice. There are those who argue that consistent underfunding builds character and is likely to weed out unserious scholars. We fear it may instead weed out those with the capacity to choose among several other attractive competing alternatives at home. In a word, we think it reasonable to presume that, with some exceptions, a lower level of compensation is likely to attract a lower level of scholarly quality to the overseas experience. In recent years the precipitous decline of the dollar against most of the major world currencies only makes matters worse.

Associated with the low and declining levels of compensation for international experience is a high level of uncertainty and confusion about the financial opportunities available. Potential applicants complained to us frequently that they could not find in any one place a complete directory of sources of funding from U.S. public agencies, private foundations, foreign governments, and other donors. Worst of all, applicants report, is the opaque character of the selection process. When they fail at the National Science Foundation (NSF), the National Endowment for the Humanities (NEH), or the National Institutes of Health (NIH), they say, they receive the peer review statements that tell them why. When they fail in the search for funds for international exchange, they usually receive no feedback, and they never know if the rejection is for personal, scholarly, political, or other reasons.

Finally, applicants complained of the extended time period between initial application and final awards (or rejections) for international projects. This delay, coupled with the need to keep many other balls in the air while putting a minimal funding package together, often doomed a scholar's plan.

Above all, we heard repeated pleas for more flexibility in international fellowship programs. A wide variety of special needs of applicants should be looked at sympathetically, from extra insurance to write-up time on return. Most important, the time period of the award should be adjusted to the special needs and circumstances of the varied applicants and not stretched to procrustean lengths. Given great financial stringency, it is necessary to adjust to other opportunities abroad (such as teaching) that may pay travel and maintenance but limit the months spent on research. Prohibitions on multiple funding sources are counterproductive to the ultimate objective of getting faculty abroad. One response to financial stringency by the donor agency should be to allocate available funds to those projects where the payoff is greatest. This may be for awards of only a few months – or even weeks – that hold the promise of high return. One prominent faculty specialist on Soviet domestic politics told us, "At this stage in my career all I need or can afford is a few weeks in the Soviet Union at one time. No award is fashioned for me to meet this objective." It seems to almost everyone that the other obstacles to foreign experience pale before the financial problems.

A university administrator pointed out to us that U.S. scholars have little knowledge of foreign funding sources, both educational institutions and private and public agencies, and they miss many opportunities through ignorance of where and how to apply and how to identify the locus of decision making.

Institutional rules and practices

Many customs and regulations of colleges and universities stand as effective barriers to the vigorous flow of faculty overseas. Some of these were constructed or accumulated over the years without thought about their impact on international exchange.

Others were formed quite consciously to accomplish that result. Those in positions of leadership within an institution wishing to increase the international experience of their faculty would do well to reflect on these practices, structures, and conditions before attempting to do anything else. We are not suggesting that change in this area is easy; indeed, it often involves reconstruction not unlike the repositioning of a cemetery. But it may be the key to dealing with the problem.

Most of the relevant practices and rules operate upon the incentive structures faced by faculty members. These reflect the rhythm and customs of the system of appointment, promotion, and tenure. In essence the problem is that, because of the rules, no point in an academic career is just right for an international experience. The escalator upward just keeps moving, and someone who steps off may not easily find a way back on. In personal and family terms the years right after graduate school are probably the most satisfactory for a period overseas, when scholar and spouse have fewest attachments, financial needs, and responsibilities and greatest flexibility, energy, and enthusiasm for dealing with innumerable challenges. But these are also the years when scientists must take postdoctoral fellowships and build up a research group, and humanists and social scientists must turn out publications at prescribed rates and build a scholarly reputation. There are also alliances to be made, fences to be mended, and even backs to be scratched. To be absent from campus for extended periods during the seven to ten years after a first appointment is unquestionably to take a high-stakes gamble, except perhaps in a relatively few fields and specialties where foreign experience is absolutely required. As someone put it to us, "You are expected to earn your stripes on the base." Even in departments that are inherently sympathetic to overseas travel, the young scholar during the early years is unusually susceptible to prejudices from other departments that are represented on promotion and tenure committees.

After tenure has been achieved, the conditions for travel are only slightly improved. A job is assured on return from abroad, but there is still promotion to full professor ahead, and by now the

children are in school and reluctant to leave their friends, basket-
ball practice, and preparation for SATs. All of these difficulties to
the contrary notwithstanding, many still think this posttenure
point an excellent career juncture for an international experience.
As one person put it, "The tenure process is just a treadmill, and a
period overseas can help the addled victim to stand upright
again."

Once the status of full professor is achieved, it would seem, on
the surface, a good time to go abroad; by this time the scholar is
relatively untouchable by narrow-minded colleagues. But at this
stage the academic is both expensive to support and sunk into a
welter of creature comforts that make leaving painful. Moreover
first-time overseas experience at this point in life can be deeply
traumatic. Linguistic adaptability is at a minimum, health may be
dicey, and spousal careers well established.

Related to the inconvenient rhythm of academic life for international experience is the prevailing skeptical attitude found
throughout academe toward what occurs overseas. U.S. higher
education is wedded to the notion of lifelong specialization and to
the conception of a lockstep career path. You are hired as an
elementary particle physicist, a South Asia historian, or a clinical
psychologist, not as a "scholar." If you veer from the predicted
career paths of these specialties, you are suspected of dilettan-
tism or sloth. Going abroad for a reason other than the pursuit of
a specific research accomplishment in your designated field is
highly suspicious in itself. But if you talk about working in other
fields of scholarship (especially in someone else's province), you
are showing signs of eccentricity bordering on irresponsibility.
Yet this straying from the paths of righteousness is exactly what
happens to many faculty who spend time abroad, and it is this
that brings them high intellectual benefits. They step softly side-
ways rather than straight ahead and usually are penalized profes-
sionally for it. We heard from a physicist about how he took to
the history of science, from a mathematician who moved to
teacher education, from a classicist who took up ethnography.
And all, despite their excitement about new stimulation and intellectual challenges, had tales of woe from the negative reactions of

their old colleagues to their unprogrammed ventures over the academic fence. They reported also outrage from those in the fields in which they were now "poaching." Usually when they returned home, they found they were unable to use their recently acquired offbeat knowledge either in the curriculum of their own department or elsewhere.

Even for those who use time overseas to pursue what are conceived to be their legitimate tasks, a host of institutional and departmental regulations stand in their way. The granting of sabbatical leaves, if they are offered at all, often does not afford enough time for adequate planning, especially where the leaves are bestowed competitively on a few rather than as a right of all who have served their time. Where salary savings from the absent faculty are recaptured by a dean or provost, the department has no, or few, funds to make up for departures, and colleagues must bear the burdens – not always with good grace. A typical arrangement at many places we visited was the dean's recapturing a minimum of one-half the salary savings while returning as little as the wages of a teaching assistant. One of the presumed punishments, or marks of atonement, for departures abroad described at several institutions is the burdening of a returnee with high teaching loads and numerous committees; this adds to the frustration of not having sufficient time to write up research results. The problems of leaving and returning seemed to be greatest for those lodged in small academic units. "When I go away," said one person in a four-person college department, "that's a loss of one quarter of the available resources." Obviously, some of the institutional conditions that discourage the gaining of foreign experience, such as rules governing sabbatical leaves and salary recapture, are easier to change than others, such as the inflexibilities of small-scale operation.

Finally, we heard complaints both about the lack of institutional planning against which to arrange personal plans and about the frequent and bewildering changes in priorities that occurred in many colleges and universities, as well as in the federal government. The pride some institutions take in not planning, we were told, permits them to shift priorities with blinding speed in response to national fashion. "No sooner have I adjusted to a Caribbean Basin Initiative," one faculty member told us, "then we're off to the Pacific Rim." Without consistency in institutional plans, faculty are unable easily to match their efforts overseas to institutional objectives.

Inevitably the incentives and disincentives for foreign study are closely linked to those for professional development as a whole. Many faculty are deeply bitter at what they perceive to be narrow-minded institutional attitudes that tend to place everything other than on-campus teaching and research in the category of "personal benefit." Certainly faculty listen closely for signals on this subject. Signals come from various points in the stratosphere of institutional management. The legislature in one state we visited had refused to sanction off-campus sabbaticals at the public institutions on the ground that, although these might be of value to the individual, they would be of no institutional significance. Conceptually they would be "equivalent to gratuities to waiters or cab drivers and therefore proscribed." The signals were certainly unambiguous in this case.

Apart from institutional structures that condition the work incentives of faculty, the academic calendar can also have an impact on the feasibility of foreign travel. The "Jan. plan" of Hampshire College and other institutions, providing for a short winter term and other innovative sequences, affects faculty as well as student mobility. The Colorado College Block Plan, under which courses are taught intensively one course at a time over three and a half weeks, seems made for short-term excursions abroad. As one faculty member told us in Colorado Springs, "Everybody is always going somewhere." The potential impact on overseas travel should certainly be taken into account in any calendar reform.

Features of the national scene

Academic travelers described various characteristics of the national *gestalt* that they felt inhibited their overseas activities and those of others. Rising above all others was the prejudice against international travel inherent in American culture. This is manifest in many features of academic life, for example, in the customary provision in grants and contracts from government agencies that international travel requires special approval. We visited several states where use of public funds was prohibited outright for travel outside the national borders. This led to ridiculous and humiliating stratagems, such as buying two tickets, one, with state funds, to the airport nearest the border, and a second, with private funds, to the wide world beyond. More important than the inconvenience of such arrangements is the message of reinforcement that goes out to those colleagues and others who nourish vestigial skepticism that any international project is not really respectable and worthwhile after all.

A second national characteristic that is alleged to serve as a barrier to international travel is an American propensity not to take cultural differences seriously. This position is consistent with the belief in the melting pot: If you boil people a little in the pot, the argument goes, they will all look approximately the same, and therefore you need not recall the distinctions with which they began. One consequence of this belief is that it makes Americans unwilling to spend very much to understand others. It just doesn't seem a good use of funds. Even when it is conceded that such understanding might be highly valuable for the economy, there persists a faith that what needs to be known can be gained quickly, easily, and at very low cost: "We've got to psych out those Japanese. We had better send a three-week mission over there!" Even a complex national policy like export promotion in other countries is thought to be understandable through lessons drawn from the United States. The particularities of other countries just don't matter much. Certain features of other societies are admitted to be inexplicable in conventional terms, but these are treated as a "black box" that, for practical purposes, may be left safely unopened.

Third, we often heard laments that at many levels U.S. society has not made the necessary institutional adjustments to enable its people to know the world. An immediately pressing problem is found in two-career families. The academics in the partnership may experience many difficulties in arranging to get away, for the reasons described above. But for the partner, employed in a large corporation or in a profession, absence for an extended period is probably close to impossible. We heard of one enlightened large corporation closely associated with a major university that had provided routinely for unpaid leaves for its employees to permit spouses to accompany academics on leave. This seemed a singularly sensible policy that could be emulated by other corporations.

Finally some academics complain that dwelling in a superpower makes traveling abroad too often a complex political statement. They are not so much objecting to any foreign policy position of the United States as bemoaning the fact that by going overseas they became hostage (literally in some cases) to forces over which they have no control. They were speaking here not so much about difficulties they encountered abroad as about problems at home. Archeologists, for example, talked of the shame they have had to bear in the United States for wanting to work in South Africa, Chile, or some Arab countries. Added complexities were created when foreign policies changed suddenly and countries to which visits had been planned for a long time fell suddenly out of favor. Once again, the complaint was not with the policies but with the problems of being an overseas scholar from a country whose policies matter so much in the world.

Conditions overseas

The longest list of obstacles to travel relates to conditions a traveler finds abroad. Many of the problems are old and familiar, related to language, housing, diet, and the education and day care of children. In addition, the libraries are often hard to use, and the laboratories antiquated. One electrical engineer reported that he melted his contact lenses in front of his foreign class because he was not accustomed to 240 v. Another scholar, who spent time in West Africa, could not, because of local bureaucratic red tape, obtain approval to conduct his research until the last day of his eight-week stay; he was relegated instead to sunning on the beach. But other complaints were new, or at least increasing in intensity. The difficulties here came from two points of origin.

First, in many countries the U.S. scholar is not welcomed in anything like the same warm fashion of the years immediately after World War II. There are several reasons for this decline in favor. The changed image of the United States, from the shining city on a hill to the declining superpower with its own axes to grind, tends to reflect on its scholars. At extremes some academics are accused of intelligence activities, whereas others are merely treated with unfriendliness or reserve, depending on events in the world at the time.

But beyond the reflected light of U.S. foreign policy is a more complex suspicion of what the visiting scholar is up to. This is especially true with area studies. In the postwar years many former colonies proudly welcomed joint participation with area studies specialists from the United States in a cooperative endeavor to understand themselves better and to solve the problems of a new nation. As the years passed, in some places what had been seen as collaboration became perceived as cultural imperialism. Under this model the U.S. scholar is an intellectual exploiter who zips in among the natives, gathers data, and zips out, winning fame and fortune at home. Many of those with whom we talked think there is a good deal of truth in this new model, reinforced by the "ugly American" syndrome. The negative attitude of non-Americans toward U.S. scholars who wish to study them is partly due to the suspicion that somehow the results may be used to increase economic, political, and social dependence or even spread U.S. domination. As one Indonesian temporarily in this country told us: "I do not want you to understand me. If you understand me, you are better equipped to dominate me. I am delighted to work with you in the cooperative search for solutions to common problems, but not in a collaborative approach to my problems." One area studies specialist was informed by one of his in-country acquaintances: "I do not wish to be part of your data set."

As a result of the less flattering picture of the U.S. academic visitor in recent years, cooperation is often withheld, grudgingly given, or constrained in complex ways that may be quite subtle. It is now common in many countries for permits to be issued for the conduct of research by foreign scholars, in effect requiring the approval of the local scholarly community. To obtain approval, joint authorship is often encouraged with local scholars.

Most of the faculty who reported the changed attitude toward their scholarly activities abroad did not deplore the change. In many cases they sympathized with the new policies and found them fair and reasonable. What they regretted was their own unpreparedness to deal with these policies and the reluctance of their stay-at-home colleagues in the United States to recognize the new obstacles and to tolerate the time taken to cope with them. One anthropologist told us that routinely in Latin America she is expected to help her hosts prepare grant proposals as the price of their cooperation. She finds this fair enough, but it is not appreciated as a legitimate research cost either by her university or by the staffs of funding agencies, who expect her to be conducting fieldwork every minute of every day.

The hesitance of foreign scholars to provide U.S. scholars unquestioning access to their research materials appears to apply in the natural sciences as well as in the social sciences and humanities. Biologists and foresters told us that whereas they used to buzz in and buzz out with their specimens, now before doing so they must learn about and respect the local culture.

A second problem in many host countries, in addition to the changed attitude toward visiting scholars, is the widespread increase of bureaucratic impediments to scholarly activity, both in higher education and elsewhere in society. The same problem exists with different manifestations in our own society, but it reaches critical levels abroad. We heard dozens of tales of long waits for visas, police clearances, and permits of every kind. A general observation is that nothing ever seems to get done as expected. Libraries and museums turn out to be closed unexpectedly, campuses in turmoil, communications blocked. One scientist told us of looking wistfully at the equipment he had brought with him, still in its crates in the customs shed of his host country as he boarded the plane to leave after a year in residence. Once again, however, beyond a certain amount of ventilation and teeth-gnashing we detected less anger at these conditions among U.S. scholars than hope that something could be done to deal with them. Several persons suggested that at the beginning of the 1990s the U.S. government should make more of a contribution to the quality of educational experiences abroad by weighing in on some of these problems. One pointed out that this was a strong reason for the United States to rejoin UNESCO. Appreciating the close link of faculty interchange to competitiveness and economic and social vigor, federal agencies should be able to help smooth the path of scholars overseas just as they smooth those of business people and diplomats.

Many thoughtful observers of international educational exchange believe several of the problems of overseas scholars could be alleviated, if not eliminated, by higher levels of understanding on both sides. A great deal of emphasis was placed on adequate preparation and communication at both ends of the flow.

6

Issues for debate

Unlike some other topics in international education, such as the place of area studies in the curriculum and the costs and benefits of foreign students and study abroad, the importance of an international experience for U.S. faculty has not received focused attention either on the U.S. campus or at the level of public policy formation. Partly this reflects the lack of a convenient niche or category through which to remind all concerned of the subject's importance. There is seldom an administrator responsible for the process on a campus, there is no national association to worry about it, and there is no place in government to review it in all its dimensions. In consequence the level of discourse on the subject is often superficial and disorganized, or nonexistent.

In this chapter we set forth for discussion issues that deserve the attention of thoughtful people both on the campuses and in public decision-making positions at the state and national levels. These lists draw upon the material already discussed.

Questions for the campus

1. Does it matter?

This question, like most others, must inevitably be answered differently for different campuses and for various parts of any campus. That is because objectives and values vary, as do appraisals of local, regional, national, and global circumstances. It is important, however, to face these objectives and circumstances squarely, to examine thoroughly the relevance of faculty experience, and not to allow the settling of significant questions by default.

The first matter to explore is the set of standards by which an institution judges itself. Does the institution attempt to stand at the forefront of the disciplines it addresses, or is it prepared to accept a less exalted rank? Is its objective, perhaps, to educate large numbers of the state's or a center city's youths, or does it aim at a mature adult constituency? Does it propose to inculcate the values of a church? Does it serve a social class? Institutional rhetoric may point misleadingly to an inapplicable objective. Before one can explore the possible value of international exchange, one needs a candid understanding of the objective that applies.

Some examples will illustrate alternative policies. On the one hand, a public university charged principally with teaching and conducting research on a range of applied areas of concern to a state may find most critical the development of rich international faculty relationships in those applied fields where the scholarly frontiers lie, or are rapidly moving, overseas. Its priorities will lead it toward collegial relationships with applied scientists and scientific institutions abroad that will strengthen its capacity to meet its specific set of obligations at home. In contrast, a small liberal arts college may be willing to stand well back from the research frontier, focusing instead on inspired teaching and paying little attention to the kind of product-oriented professional interaction valued by the public university.

A different set of values and objectives, however, will impel a small college to send its faculty abroad with as great a sense of urgency as a large one's. For example, one college's commitment to sustaining and periodically reinvigorating the intellectual performance of its teachers may be most effectively met through an overseas experience. Another college, regretting the tendency in U.S. academic life for areas of knowledge to gravitate increasingly into separate boxes, may turn to an international experience, which, by throwing faculty together with nondepartmental colleagues, by opening up new scholarly questions for attack, and by forcing contact with a different academic culture, may help to change intellectual perspectives back home and release the forces needed to combat intellectual fragmentation. Alternatively, a third small college could find that the promotion of faculty experiences abroad helps achieve its goal of internationalizing its curriculum; unquestionably, faculty who have served abroad are more sympathetic to this curricular reform.

Another example is found in the many U.S. institutions of higher learning that are located in geographically isolated locations. Both students and faculty can become "stir crazy" after extended periods on campus. Study abroad for students has been developed consciously by some of these institutions as a compensatory device. The same approach can be taken by the college toward faculty, yielding a highly specialized justification for an overseas experience.

Finally, a major, multifaceted, research-oriented university may encourage faculty exchange because it perceives most problems as global and the appropriate community through which to solve these as all of humankind. Isolation from the rest of the world for any of the faculty in these conditions is fundamentally inconsistent with institutional objectives.

These are only examples of ways in which an international experience by faculty may serve varied institutional goals. The point is that the justification for stimulating or supporting such an experience can be constructed only when the ultimate objectives and the links to these objectives are well specified and understood. It is possible to conceive in theory but difficult to imagine in practice an institution that would not benefit at all from faculty experience abroad. The real questions for the 1990s are how many the benefits and how great the costs.

2. Planning and implementation – the iron fist or the invisible hand?

The question about which we heard by far the most vehement declamations in our conversations with faculty members concerned the means by which the leadership of a campus could legitimately, and indeed should, promote the international experience of its faculty. We found the issue resting on the answers to two questions upon which people understandably differ. The first question is whether the benefits for the educational community derived from faculty members gaining international experience are sufficient to justify encouragement by this community. Moreover, can faculty be effectively stimulated to greater international involvement by some modest financial support and facilitation, or is some kind of central planning mechanism required? The academic community is accustomed to facilitating the attendance of faculty at professional meetings through the reimbursement of travel expenses, and it insists upon continuing faculty participation in scholarly life by making publication a requirement for professional advancement. Clearly the community is agreed that the communal benefits of these two activities justify subsidy in one case and punitive enforcement in the other. Is the gaining of international experience by faculty equivalent to these two activities where the existence of community interest, rather than simply personal benefit, is seldom questioned? An unambiguous answer to this question is difficult because of the complexity of the benefits that emerge and by reason of their distribution among the teaching, research, and faculty development dimensions of the institution.

The first question is whether, when a faculty member goes abroad, it benefits the scholarly community or just the scholar in question. The second question is whether even the generation of substantial, acknowledged community benefits can justify the social and political costs of some measure of intervention by college and university administrations. (Some called this "leadership," others "inspiration," still others "tyranny.") Feelings usually run exceptionally high on this issue, with a few (usually administrators) vehemently arguing for central intervention and others (mainly faculty) just as strongly rejecting it. One faculty member reminded us that he and many of his colleagues had entered academic life and made the attendant sacrifices to avoid planning and control. He favored action by central adminstration only if it "opened doors rather than closed them." Another defended the absence of administrative intervention on all matters in his in-

stitution as "natural academic equilibrium" wherein patterns
emerged spontaneously. The important observation here is that
many faculty we interviewed considered subsidies to foreign experience an unwarranted intervention, but institutional support
for domestic travel quite right and proper. How to change these
attitudes is far from clear.

On the spectrum of what might be done by an administration,
from nothing ("Let the invisible hand of markets work its will"),
on the one side, to specific direction ("It's your turn to go to
Chad, Charlie; get packed"), on the other, a variety of things can
be done or are being done on various campuses. A theoretical
possibility that, we confess, we never saw in effect would have
the campus community, either through its executive leadership or
through the organs of faculty government, prepare and implement
some form of strategic planning with respect to its international
dimension. This might involve identifying goals, reviewing resources, and selecting activities so that they would complement
each other. An institution might decide, for example, to direct its
international activities primarily toward one world region, say,
Latin America. Area studies, language training, technical assistance, foreign students, study abroad, and faculty travel would be
given a Latin American "tilt." It would seem that area studies,
language specialization, technical assistance contracts, and student and faculty exchange programs might contribute much to
each other. In fact, however, we found that almost everywhere
these various international programs had grown up virtually by
serendipity and without respect to each other. We, as faculty
members on our own campuses, appreciate and benefit from the
liberty (or as some would have it, the anarchy) that is so much
treasured on the U.S. campus. Nevertheless, we wonder if perhaps freedom cannot sometimes be purchased at too high a price
and if some coherent strategy and some planning structure might
not yield high rewards. Although we saw few cases of dynamic
leadership by senior academic administrators on the question of
internationalization, we saw enough to be persuaded that much
may be accomplished thereby. An effective leader may dramatize
the issue, identify salient features, and clarify options. And by

bringing along academic followers voluntarily, a successful leader need not infringe liberties to excess.

One limited approach to planning is to make it supplementary to what individual campus entrepreneurs are doing anyway. If an institution decides collectively, for example, that it should concentrate on East Asia, it can direct hard-funds encouragement to area studies, foreign students, study abroad, and faculty exchange with that region. It need not discourage efforts by individual faculty with soft money in other directions. We must point out that on the majority of campuses on which we tried out this idea it was soundly rejected by faculty on the ground that it conflicted with principles of academic freedom and required action by a central administration that was incompetent and could not be trusted. This being said, we think still that coordinated action on this critical subject by the academic community is most desirable. The result of absence of institutional planning is not necessarily some blessed social equilibrium wherein everyone's interest is taken into account. It is more likely that external agents, such as government, foundations, or corporations, will establish priorities for the institution. We visited one major university where the focus on particular foreign countries betrayed no discernible logic: area studies in the Middle East, languages and culture of Latin America, study abroad in Western Europe, foreign students from East Asia, and technical assistance to Africa. When we delved into the history of the institution, we found that this crazy quilt could be explained only by the vagaries of government funding over the years, which had left its shadow in the pattern of this institution's internationalization. The result was not catastrophic, but it was assuredly suboptimal and stood in the way of most synergisms that would have emerged from coordinated development.

Between tight planning and complete laissez-faire there are steps that a central administration can take to encourage the international experience of faculty. It can, for example, provide for a coordinating director or dean of international programs or, at a minimum, an adviser with access to information about options. It can raise funds and enlist the cooperation of alumni. It can, like one provost we met, lean into the winds of fashion so as to stabilize the campus situation; he supports travel to Europe when the Pacific Rim is hot and to the Third World when national priorities shift toward the socialist countries. Indeed, he argued that this is the job of the provost: "We have had traditional strength in East Asian and Soviet studies. We'll always have resources in these areas because senior distinguished faculty see to it that this is so. My job is to provide support in areas where this is not the case." Alternatively, the leadership can, like that at another university, engage "exchange finders" in other countries, who line up opportunities overseas that are essentially retailed at home.

It is widely conceded that the rapidly increasing corps of foreign alumni of U.S. higher education are not effectively integrated into the continuing lives of the institutions. Recruitment of these alumni for assistance to faculty overseas is a function that the institutional leaders should consider undertaking. It can engage the local business community as well to provide direct assistance, contacts abroad, and sympathy for leaves of absence to spouses of would-be academic travelers.

One place today where the issue of international sophistication among faculty may come up against the planning process is over the contemporary pressure for undergraduate curricular revision. If, for example, a decision is made to introduce more non-western material to the core curriculum (as was the recent experience at Stanford University), the authorities have the clear responsibility to deliver faculty who are suitably equipped to handle the teaching tasks. Short of recruiting a new corps of faculty, the nurturing and retraining of those at hand may be the only practical alternative. For this, experience abroad may be an effective didactic device.

We do not wish to imply in this section either that no planning occurs on U.S. campuses today or that everywhere a tight planning process per se is necessarily desirable. In some places absence of planning may be a virtue. We visited one institution where, reportedly, the president, under pressure from external forces, had planned and decided to internationalize the campus but had picked a strange device to accomplish this objective:

International celebrities were invited at great cost to act as catalysts. The faculty felt alienated as a result, and the strategy backfired. The implication was clear: Bad planning is worse than none.

3. Rules and regulations

A campus community that finds itself sympathetic to the notion of faculty gaining more international experience abroad could do no better than to review the customs and conditions that may encourage or discourage this process. The following are only a few of the practices that deserve scrutiny and possible revision: limitations on funding for international travel; partial rather than full funding of sabbatical pay; refusal to top-up external awards that, alone, do not provide sufficient funds to attract first-rate applicants; penalties upon departments or schools that allow leaves, such as salary "recovery" by the central administration of faculty on leave without pay; failure to continue benefits and movement up the salary scale for faculty absent from campus; and tight restrictions on absences from campus during term, which may be required for some international experience.

One important by-product of a review and reform of institutional rules and regulations may be that institutional rhetoric about the global campus will come to correspond more closely to reality.

4. What about nonconformists?

The job descriptions of some campus citizens in effect dictate international experience: teachers of language, scholars of world civilization, specialists in comparative government. Few people on the campus doubt the legitimacy of encouragement and even assistance for them to go. Questions arise quickly, however, about those with professional and personal reasons that are more opaque, including a need to see new horizons, find stimulation and renewal, or even seek out a new field or subfield. We think it crucial for an institution to discuss openly the legitimacy of these interests and, to the degree found appropriate, give them encouragement and the benefit of the doubt.

It is not difficult to list persuasive reasons why the international travel plans of these nonconformists may be perceived as not serious and unworthy of scarce funding. The very vagueness of their objectives condemns them when contrasted with familiar justifications. Yet we found some of these nontraditional purposes suffused with freshness and excitement, and somewhere they should find a sympathetic ear. We heard, for example, from a highly persuasive biochemist who wished to conduct an examination of the "political economy" of the Chernobyl nuclear accident using her knowledge of the sciences and social sciences. She had been repeatedly rebuffed. She was guilty of the double heresy of proposing at the same time to cross fields and to enter an unfamiliar area. We recognize the dangers in rewarding nonconformity; mere novelty may be empty. At the same time we sense opportunities. This kind of academic travel may be the route to the intellectual frontier.

The most pronounced nonconformists among would-be international travelers today are those who would combine the perspectives of two or more disciplines and/or the experience of two or more regions of the world. Many of the structures and institutions of academic life are designed to impede such adventuresomeness. Funds are granted by economists for economists, by Japanologists for Japanologists. We believe this situation should be corrected.

Issues at the national level

1. Relationship to national goals

It is quite possible to conceive of some international experiences of faculty that are valuable to the home institutions, and therefore worthy of support by these institutions, but are not of any particular national significance, and therefore without justification for national support. But there are many faculty experiences where this is not the case. We see four reasons, at a minimum, why the nation should, indeed, pay attention to and assist faculty travel. All of these have been taken into account by various government programs to different degrees at different times in the past.

The first reason is that a sophisticated community of well-traveled scholars of international affairs is a valuable national resource by which this country may understand other nations, both friendly and unfriendly, and the processes by which international relations take place and are changing. One need only reflect on the number of assistants to the president for national security affairs who came from academe (for example, McGeorge Bundy, Walt Rostow, Henry Kissinger, Zbigniew Brzezinski), as well as innumerable other public servants and participants in the policy debate. The function of the well-informed academic is especially important in the United States, where the cadre of professional diplomats-public servants have worked in tandem with such academics at the ear of presidents and leaders of Congress. Such programs of the federal government as those funded under Title VI of the Higher Education Act (for Language and Area Studies) are implicitly aimed at the development of this kind of skilled professional competence.

Second, scholarly interchange is widely perceived to be a means whereby the very relations among nations are forged, understood, and often improved. Although it is hard to prove conclusively, it can be argued persuasively that scholarly contacts with both friends and adversaries since World War II have reduced misperceptions, at a minimum, and in some cases have suggested means to achieve positive improvement in relations. The Fulbright program was established in part for this purpose, as have been more narrowly targeted exchanges with the Soviet Union, China, Japan, and other nations.

Third, the scholarly community has been employed since World War II as one of the most effective contracting agents to assist the development efforts of Third World nations. Academics have been employed both to provide direct training and to contribute to the improvement of Third World educational systems. They have also participated in development projects of all kinds, from crop improvement to economic planning. That experienced, internationally sophisticated U.S. universities are best able to take part in development assistance is evidenced by the tendency of assistance agencies to direct the bulk of their contracts to a relatively few highly experienced U.S. universities. These agencies have become increasingly conscious (as in the provision of AID Title XII funds) of the relevance to their own effectiveness of the intellectual health and welfare of these contracting institutions.

The fourth reason for national attention to faculty experience abroad relates to the importance of science to the economy and the contribution that international science may make to domestic productivity. There has long been some recognition of this contribution, for example, in federal support for international activities of American scientists through the foreign secretary of the National Academy of Sciences (NAS) and international programs of the NSF. But overall we discern the prevailing view of international science at the federal level as dictating some attention to the less fortunate nations and also facilitating the maintenance of scientific networks through conferences, some collaborative programs, and the exchange of research results. We are not aware of any serious attention to the kind of subtle nurturing of bilateral international scientific links – especially lacking in applied areas, where the United States is behind – of the kind we heard discussed often on campuses (reported in Chapter 2). The rejuvenation of the president's science advisory office, endorsed by both presidential candidates in 1988, could further this nurturing.

We think that all four reasons for national attention to the internationalization of U.S. scholarship remain valid, but we think their meaning and dimensions have changed considerably since they were first recognized, in most cases shortly after World War II. We think the time is ripe indeed for thoughtful reexamination of all four reasons at the national level and for adjustment of federal programs to a modern appraisal of their current legitimacy.

2. Institutional support structures

A strong impression we took away from our conversations with college and university faculty and administrations was that it is high time for a serious and bold reconstruction of the mechanisms at the national level for the support of international scholarly experience. Most of these were put in place several decades ago, and in part at least, events have passed them by. The kinds of public support for time abroad that are available at the moment are roughly as follows: fellowships allocated by peer review for extended periods of research or teaching overseas under the Fulbright program, Fulbright-Hays Title VI, the National Endowments for the Arts and Humanities, and various intermediary bodies, such as the American Institute of Indian Studies; short-term lecture tours arranged by USIA, Department of State, or other governmental sponsors; participation in developmental projects under contract, principally with AID; and attendance at international conferences and congresses paid for by the several research funding agencies, including NIH and NSF. In addition, the major private foundations provide travel support for a variety of purposes, mostly but not entirely for ad hoc research and conferences.

Admirable as these modes are, and recognizing that they should continue with at least their present vigor, it appears that none of them takes account adequately of certain conditions that prevail in modern academe, in particular (1) the need for many short-term visits, often on brief notice, because of the greater number of experienced mature scholars in the United States who no longer require the extensive period in residence and find long-term visits impractical, (2) the need for continuing collaborative exchange relationships overseas, especially in the sciences, that may ripen over an extended period of years and cannot be well served by a series of unrelated ad hoc visits, (3) the reality of immensely fast-paced modern communication and transportation, changing travel needs, and (4) the personal problems of long-term travel that the two-career family symbolizes. To what extent have the traditional year-long, or even semester-long or quarter-long, visits become obsolete when visitors are faced with circumstances that have changed so dramatically from the 1940s and 1950s when they were conceived? Moreover, is the pursuit of various national goals still well served by the distinctly separate vehicles of the Fulbright fellowship, Title VI, the AID contract,

the USIA AMPART speakers' program, and others? Are not the
accomplishments of time spent abroad becoming less obviously
identified with specific objectives of particular programs? (For
example, are not some AID-supported relationships serving U.S.
scholarship through intellectual refreshment at least as much as
they are benefiting the intended Third World beneficiaries?) One
admittedly disgruntled veteran of repeated tussles with individual
national funding agencies ventured to suggest that their present
character made them as obsolete as dinosaurs. Together, he admitted, they remained enormously valuable. But by each insisting
on pursuing particular goals specified decades before, and implementing rules and bureaucratic procedures developed long ago,
they confused and impeded the well-intentioned scholarly traveler. He spoke of "ghastly and discouraging application routines,
with eighteen months of lead time and endless forms to complete." Another commented that the application process had been
for her a "bad dream." She was compelled to reconstitute her
own goals to accord with what she believed were the anachronistic objectives of the various funding agencies.

Undoubtedly the most important issue to rethink about virtually all national programs of assistance to international travel is
the highly significant decline in real funding per capita. The decline is visible not only in stipend levels, but in preparatory and
follow-up programs as well. Clearly this decline has been a calculated response to overall budget stringency. Nevertheless the full
effects must be taken into account. The situation today is that
stipends are equivalent to market rates of return for academics
only in the most exceptional circumstances. This limits programs
like Fulbright to several categories of scholar:

(a) Those who are willing to make a financial sacrifice – the
    missionary
(b) Those who can afford to make a financial sacrifice – the
    rich
(c) Those at the beginning of a career, whose regular sal-
    aries are low *and* can afford to go away, in terms of
    career security – the young

(d) Those at the end of a career – the retired or near-retired
(e) Those whom the market (their employers) compensates
    less than their fellows – the unselected
(f) Those at institutions that can afford to subsidize such
    awards – the privileged.

By and large this list excludes the highly successful, widely influential, midcareer scholar with a range of other options. This condition has prevailed now for at least a decade, and the nation has already lost a generation of this category of scholar, who should have spent time abroad in his or her prime. One engineer, about to retire and recently returned from a Fulbright, illustrated the situation well when he spoke of his regret that this "high point of his career" had happened only at the end, when he could afford to take it. A case may be made for the merits of this reverse Darwinian process wherein the most distinguished stay home, but the case needs to be weighed heavily against the costs and alternatives. We appreciate that more selective programs bear the cost of fewer persons chosen and the charge of elitism, but the benefits of assisting more highly qualified persons should not be discarded lightly. A long-term cost of below-market stipend levels bears on the reputation of a program as well as on its impact. We were sorry to hear one group of scholars refer to the Fulbright program as an "orphan."

Several insiders pointed out to us that other countries have appointed at the national level facilitators of bilateral educational exchange, whether through public or private funds. These persons perfect models, negotiate exchange relationships, and smooth the way for an easy international flow of scholars. If funding cannot be increased nationally to allow the multilateral programs to return to their former stature, the federal government might consider assuming this facilitating function through one of its agencies now involved with the exchange process. Or perhaps this is a tailor-made challenge for the U.S. private foundation. In part the major impediment to greater scholarly flows is financial, but it is also partly a failure of imagination and the capacity to respond to new problems and opportunities. Private foundations at this juncture may perform a major service, not in financing the flow, for which they are ill equipped, but in showing the way, as they have done so successfully before in other areas.

3. A case for centralized leadership?

We appreciate in full measure the benefits of decentralized decision making. Abuses of power are curtailed where power is dispersed and authority fragmented. But there are costs to this dispersion, too. In this case, absent on the national scene is any part of government with responsibility to reflect seriously and act upon the full range of subjects discussed in this report. The case for vigorous central leadership is much stronger today than it has been heretofore. Not only is there planning and coordination to conduct on the domestic scene, but the more complex and sometimes inhospitable environment faced by U.S. scholars overseas calls for aggressive centralized negotiations. To make this point more constructively, if U.S. scholars are to benefit to the full from their international experiences in the future, it may be necessary not only for their national government to defend their interests aggressively, but also for this government to arrange for a service dimension to their presence when they are researchers and a research dimension when they are assistance personnel, making reciprocal benefits possible. The objectives and accomplishments of the Fulbright program, AID, NSF, and innumerable other agencies in assisting U.S. faculty to go overseas should not be treated separately and apart.

Where a central coordinating and implementing agency should be located we do not presume to suggest. But in its absence, we fear, many opportunities will be lost, and matters important to the nation's welfare will fall through the cracks.

4. Should the nation lead the campus?

Our discussion to this point had tended to picture the questions for decision as resting at the two levels – campus and federal government. A more complex question is whether appropriate standards should be determined at the national level and then enforced by the carrot or the stick on the campus. In particular, some with whom we talked suggested that national fellowship programs like Fulbrights might be used to compel individual campuses to act "responsibly" toward winners. A list of conditions could be compiled, to which the trustees and president of a campus would be required to accede if its faculty members were to be considered for awards. These conditions would become more acceptable, of course, if the national awards were more generous and prestigious. They might include a requirement for some kind of institutional matching, either in the form of salary or reduced institutional responsibilities during a postaward write-up period, the option of stopping the tenure clock during the fellowship (a step that has been taken voluntarily by a number of institutions, but remains highly controversial in most others), uninterrupted cost-of-living and merit pay increases during the fellowship period, and general facilitation of the overseas departure through the flexible continuation of health care and other fringe benefits. The legitimacy of such external intervention, of course, goes right to the heart of the appropriate relationship between a college or university and the community in which it lives. Our overall judgment, however, is that the current set of laissez-faire relationships is inadequate to the task at hand.

7

Case studies

As we have recounted in earlier chapters, the overseas experiences of faculty serve a multitude of important purposes on the U.S. campus. In this chapter we illustrate these varied uses by summarizing a set of imaginative programs at five colleges and universities wherein faculty experience abroad was the decisive mechanism used to achieve a well-defined end.

Global Awareness Program of Wheaton College

Wheaton is a small, high-quality liberal arts college in southern Massachusetts with a distinguished record of service to women that goes back well into the nineteenth century. However, as Wheaton entered the 1980s it faced a variety of serious problems. Alice Emerson, Wheaton's president, recognized that broad-gauged internationalization of the entire college community was essential because of increasing international interdependence and the need to educate for global citizenship. It seemed to her that the times dictated it. Her sensitivity to the opportunity was heightened by a trip to China in 1980, after which she was deeply impressed by the extent to which American students, despite the availability at Wheaton and elsewhere of conventional language, area study, and study abroad programs, remained largely ignorant of non-Western cultures. She perceived the chance to pursue a course that was both pedagogically sound and responsive to the particular needs of the college.

President Emerson concluded that change in the level of international awareness in a college community must begin among the faculty. Moreover, she came to believe that a dramatic transformation in faculty awareness and sensitivity could be achieved by brief periods abroad. In her "Memorandum to Members of the Faculty" (October 29, 1982) she wrote: "Based on my own and others' experience, I am convinced that relatively short exposures to other cultures (one-to-three months) can be an extremely effective means for expanding one's awareness." With support from trustees, alumnae, and the Exxon Education Foundation, she began the Faculty Overseas Internship Program, under which faculty members are sent to non-Western countries for periods ranging from four to eight weeks. The faculty go as learners to the foreign country, with specific prearranged internship assignments. The goal was to enhance global awareness on the campus, to infuse a broader awareness and interest in international affairs, particularly relating to non-Western countries, into the learning environment for *all* students. In the selection of interns "Priority is given to a person who knows less about a country, but shows an interest in working in a new culture and facing the difficulties of being away from the security of his or her specialty." Some orientation is provided for interns. The internships are operated in a most frugal fashion, each costing only a few thousand dollars.

By the end of 1987 eighteen faculty members (one-fifth of all faculty) had participated in the internship program, spending time in South Korea, Thailand, Kenya, the Seychelles, Egypt, and Israel. A professor of chemistry was able to develop baseline data for the government of the Seychelles, enabling it to track air pollution; a professor of mathematics and computer science developed a computerized classification system for the artifacts of an archaeological dig in Israel (and has returned twice since); a poet-in-residence participated on the editorial staff of a children's magazine in Kenya; and a professor of music taught English to Thai business people. These four examples are typical of the eighteen internship experiences. All were *learning,* rather than teaching, projects. The results are difficult to specify confidently, but they appear to have been considerable and very positive. Clearly none of the faculty became country experts as a consequence of a few weeks abroad. But in most cases their outlook was substantially modified and their minds opened to discovering more. In our conversations we found that the personal experience varied widely in agreeableness and human comforts. Frustration and even anger were the result of some sojourns, but these were the result of contact with real life, rather than with an insulated world orchestrated by a tourist agent. And even many of those who were frustrated changed their approach in the classroom when they returned to campus.

In a small college even this modest investment can be felt. Almost no student can escape a class with a former faculty intern, and many now, unlike a few years ago, find a teacher of creative writing reading African poetry or a sociologist making comparisons between U.S. conditions and those in Egypt. Vigorous efforts are undertaken to make full use of the interns' experiences soon after their return. They give lectures and workshops and advise students contemplating study abroad, and they are also encouraged to interact closely with students on the Wheaton campus from the country they visited. There seems ample evidence that even brief experiences abroad by faculty have made foreign students from all countries more comfortable with their U.S. environment, realizing that their teachers have made some effort to understand the cultures from which they came.

The faculty internships are only one part of the comprehensive Global Awareness Program that President Emerson has put in place at Wheaton. Other components include expanded study abroad opportunities for students, special lecture series, visiting faculty from the Third World, and administrative support to facilitate international exchanges of various kinds. *But the faculty internships are an essential ingredient. They serve as a catalyst and stimulus to the other activities. Putting it negatively, without faculty commitment, all else would be in vain.*

It is always difficult to trace cause and effect on a campus, but the facts are that since the commencement of the faculty internships at Wheaton the number and range of countries of origin of students from abroad have increased markedly. Students are spending their junior year and internships in a wider variety of locations, programs on campus with an international focus have grown exponentially (including non-Western languages and international TV broadcasts), and faculty-led programs to developing countries have become commonplace (for example, to Ecuador and Kenya in 1989). In recognition of the enduring value of foreign experience Wheaton students are now required to take an orientation and reentry course in relation to a junior year abroad.

There seems little doubt that the Wheaton faculty internships did lead to curricular reform in some cases, to changes in values and perspectives in others, and to increased internationalization of the campus overall. A major remaining question is whether these effects are permanent or must be reinforced regularly through fresh internships. Is the Wheaton experiment to date like an inoculation against provincialism that will last a lifetime, or is it like a nutritional supplement that must be sustained? The answer to this question lies several years in the future.

Bunker Hill Community College

Bunker Hill Community College (BHCC) is a public two-year undergraduate institution founded in 1973 to serve primarily the needs of inner-city Boston. The president for fifteen years was Harold E. Shively, an educator with considerable previous international experience. President Shively believed fervently that an institution with BHCC's challenges and responsibilities could not afford provincialism in the last quarter of the twentieth century. There are three reasons why broad internationalization of the college seemed essential to him from the outset. First, since more than a third of all undergraduate student credit enrollment is in community colleges, nationwide global understanding for citizenship must in large part come from these institutions. In the words of a BHCC document, "If a student is to get some sort of international orientation, it will most likely come at the lower division undergraduate level of the student's higher educational experience. Community colleges will be the place where most undergraduate students will have an opportunity for this exposure."

Second, the New England region in the 1970s and 1980s experienced an economic boom led by export-related manufacturing that demanded greater world understanding from its work force.

Exports increased fourfold from the early 1970s, making New England by the end of the 1980s the most export intensive region of the United States, with Massachusetts in the lead. Foreign investment was equally important. There were fifteen hundred foreign firms in the area with combined assets of $5.5 billion. It was clearly impossible for skilled workers in Massachusetts either to sell abroad effectively or to work for foreign employers without having some comprehension of the languages and cultures of their economic partners. It was hazardous also to operate in a complex world economy without some grasp of the forces that buffeted the players.

Finally, and perhaps of greatest importance, BHCC was faced with a changing student population of inner-city Boston, which demanded an imaginative response. In addition to the traditional ethnic mix, there was a foreign student population with expenditures in the state estimated at $300 million annually, an immigrant population drawn by the economic opportunities, and even a substantial refugee component. By 1987 there were 267 foreign students from sixty-seven countries at BHCC and a resident alien population of almost eight hundred. From 6 percent in the college's first class, the proportion of minorities in the student body rose to 40 percent. As a college document puts it: "The definition of 'community' for BHCC has changed radically since the college's inception in 1973."

There were obvious steps that could be taken to speed along the internationalization that BHCC found to be desirable. English as a second language was offered, and the administration was reorganized to provide specific encouragement to internationally oriented activities. But two of the approaches open to large research-oriented universities were closed to BHCC, the development of high-powered area studies and technical assistance programs to Third World nations. President Shively turned instead to exchanges, of both faculty and students, as a means to accomplish greater internationalization of curriculum and the very atmosphere of the college.

The devices employed by President Shively to implement his policy of exchange were a combination of formal encouragement at the highest administrative levels and facilitation of departures lower down. BHCC took a leadership role in the formation and development of several community college consortia for study abroad, development assistance, and exchange. In all of these the means were provided for college faculty to move abroad in a variety of roles and thereby to enlarge their international perspectives. The key elements in this route to college internationalization, as we saw it, were the legitimacy, indeed, fashionableness, given to the process of gaining international experience through presidential approval and the presentation of opportunities to a community that otherwise might never have known what had been missed. Most of the interviewed faculty who had gone abroad had done so at considerable financial sacrifice (one estimated a loss of $6,000 for one semester). It is striking, therefore, that they had gone.

Where the conventional academic measures of articles published in scholarly journals, development assistance contracts gained, area studies centers created, and doctorates granted are irrelevant, as they are in a community college, success or failure of internationalization is hard to demonstrate conclusively. In our assessment we depended on conversations with community members.

The evidence was impressive. We heard extended accounts from a mathematician of a period spent in Surinam to provide training in self-paced individualized learning, a physicist exchanged places with an opposite number at a British college, another went to Melbourne, and so on. In terms of what President Shively intended to accomplish by this flow, it seemed to us that the experiences achieved his goals. Above all, the time overseas became an intense learning experience for those involved, along several dimensions. For those faculty who had never been abroad before, the impact was dizzying. Because the arrangements made for them were usually minimal, the adjustments were often traumatic. For example, one didn't know you couldn't take ten suitcases on an airplane and faced a huge excess baggage charge; another couldn't figure out how to get the gas on in his new British flat and shivered for days. But the long-term personal changes were far more important. One talked of how, for the first time, he was able to appreciate the complex filters through which others saw the United States; this gave him an entirely new perspective on his own country and made him more responsive to those students who came from different cultures. Several faculty remarked that the exchange experience in Europe had made them sensitive to the benefits of rigorous academic standards; they also learned different teaching skills, such as ways to conduct a seminar effectively and to silence obstreperous troublemakers. Several faculty remarked that the experience of teacher abroad gave them a new regard and sympathy for foreign students and resident aliens, for the skills they bring, the different viewpoints they can offer, and the adjustment problems they face.

What is especially striking about the internationalization drive at BHCC is that it has been employed to accomplish the principal objective of the institution, provision of high-quality education to an evolving student body in a changing world. No marginalism here! Moreover, the drive has been carried on without the investment of substantial internal or external funds – neither of which is readily available to a community college. Whether such progress can survive the departure of a dynamic and committed president remains to be seen. For many institutions, nevertheless, this is a model to be studied carefully.

Lewis and Clark College

In the Palantine Hill section of Portland sits the beautiful Lewis and Clark College campus. The college enjoys a solid academic reputation, with an emphasis on liberal arts education for students seeking the freedom to promote creative and critical thinking. Virtually from its founding Lewis and Clark identified international affairs as a major area of activity. This is reflected today in its programs and even in its academic calendar. International affairs is the most popular major among the student body. Roughly 3 percent of the undergraduate student body of seventeen hundred is non-American, including both immigrants and international students. The academic calendar operates on a three-term schedule: September through late November, early January through March, and April through mid-June. The schedule permits ample travel opportunities during the academic year.

Lewis and Clark has particular strengths in the social sciences and in studies of developing countries. Most of the students are preprofessionals, headed upon graduation for law and business schools, rather than for the doctoral degree. The college has a strong sabbatical leave policy, and paid leaves for nontenured faculty are reported to be plentiful. What is special about Lewis and Clark is the well-established student study abroad programs led by college faculty. A large number of such programs have long been functioning, and it is this mechanism that permits many of the faculty to spend substantial time abroad. Although research is sometimes possible, it is not the principal goal. The faculty abroad are both helping to enrich the learning experience of their students and broadening their own horizons. Unlike many institution-sponsored student study abroad programs, roughly half the Lewis and Clark students and their accompanying faculty spend time in the Third World. The trips also serve as a recruiting device to introduce non-American students to the Lewis and Clark student body. When these non-Americans ultimately enroll, they in turn can take advantage of the study abroad programs to visit and learn about other parts of the world. It is not uncommon, for example, for a student from South Asia to be part of a Lewis and Clark overseas group to the Middle East. These trips, we were convincingly told, greatly enhance the knowledge of the returning faculty, and this has been a major catalyst in transforming the curriculum into one that is explicitly non-Eurocentric.

Some of the international programs have a general cultural focus and others are more highly specialized. General culture programs have been established in Ecuador, Greece, Japan, and Kenya, and as a result of faculty experiences in these countries courses have been introduced into the curriculum that otherwise would probably have been absent. Programs with a sharper focus have included studying German language and literature in Munich and perfecting language skills in China, Costa Rica, France, Japan, and the Soviet Union. It was at Lewis and Clark that we

were told passionately of the value of the study abroad program
by a mathematician who had run out of steam intellectually and
knew he would never make the National Academy of Sciences or
publish great original mathematical research. After accompanying students to India, he became completely dedicated to a career
in creating teaching materials for instructing Third World students in mathematical concepts. This experience had a profound
effect on his teaching, research, and service to the college.

These programs are not problem free, however. We were told
of some faculty who "go abroad too often" and of the difficulty at
times in coordinating trips across departments. Funding can also
be difficult, but it has been managed successfully to date. Funds
for the faculty abroad come from the student study abroad programs (students pay an extra fee that helps defray program costs)
and from support from U.S. government agencies.

On balance, these programs appear to be a huge success.
Roughly two-thirds of the student body participate in these international experiences. Approximately 90 percent of those involved remain enrolled in the college, whereas only 60 percent of
those who do not participate are retained. Most of the programs
are organized by discipline; small numbers of students are led to
Third World countries by faculty specializing in those areas. "We
have changed the lives of more than half our students and more
than a quarter of our faculty through these programs," one senior
administrator asserted. We were convinced. These programs are
a principal focus of activity for the institution, they are of significant educational value to faculty as well as students, they have
stimulated the internationalization of the undergraduate curriculum, and they have served as a model for other institutions that
wish to go down a similar path.

University of Washington

The University of Washington is one of the nation's major comprehensive state research universities and certainly one of the
most significant academic centers in the western United States.
Situated on a lovely campus in the heart of Seattle, its more than

twenty thousand undergraduates and fifteen thousand graduate
students have before them a first-rate faculty with particular
strength in the natural sciences, Soviet and East Asian studies,
and foreign languages. In the course of our visit to the campus we
encountered numerous faculty who had been abroad under a variety of sponsorships for both research and teaching purposes. The
university, for example, has special expertise in comparative legal studies, including Japanese contract law, and law school faculty in this specialty have been routinely supported by the administration to travel abroad to stay abreast of their field. We met, as
well, with faculty associated with the Soviet and Eastern European Studies Center and the Jackson School of International
Affairs. These faculty regularly go abroad, winning Fulbright
research, IREX, and other competitive grants. This is to be
expected from a faculty of a major research university.

What was especially noteworthy, however, was our discussions with George Beckmann, who has subsequently stepped
down from the provost's position after ten years in the job. Beckmann, more than any other provost we met, articulated a philosophy and indeed a strategy for the job that included faculty study
abroad.

According to Beckmann, it is unrealistic to believe that a
provost of a major research university can have enormous influence except in a few areas: "The university is highly decentralized,
indeed often anarchical, and this is the way it should be," we were
told. Beckmann believes that the job of the provost is to select a
few high-priority areas and stick to them. In his case at Washington
he concluded some time ago that modernization of scientific facilities and the enhancement of the research libraries were at the top
of the list. Beckmann believes that the cost of conducting state-of-
the-art research in the natural sciences is so astronomical that only
ten to fifteen major universities will be in the business at the end of
this century. Washington seeks to be one of these and has developed a plan to invest almost $2 billion over the next decade to
ensure that it continues to do first-class science. Even this might
not be enough, he lamented, given that UCLA has just invested
$500 million in new scientific facilities and UC Berkeley has ex-

pended $170 million for just one biological laboratory complex. Recruiting a crackerjack director of libraries and ensuring the availability of enough quality library space are also essential to maintain an institution's research capability. Besides this focus on academic infrastructure, Beckmann argued, recruitment of aggressive deans is a top priority because it is through quality deans that first-rate department chairs and their faculty are recruited. After these, the most significant contribution a provost can make is to "bend against the wind," supporting areas of activity that would otherwise go undernourished. It is this philosophy that led Beckmann to be a major supporter of faculty experiences abroad, especially to Western Europe.

Beckmann argued that the university's historical area studies strengths were in the East Asian and Soviet fields. With the university's special location on the Pacific Rim, it is not surprising that a large variety of opportunities are available for faculty to spend time in East Asia. The productivity of scholars in the Soviet field has similarly provided easy access to funds supporting research in both the Soviet Union and Eastern Europe. What Beckmann found lacking, however, was the traditional familiarity of faculty with social science research in Western Europe, and it is in these areas that he sought to make a difference. A number of years ago Beckmann started to raise funds aggressively from private sources to promote faculty exchanges with major European universities. He did this both to strengthen social science departments and to bring to the campus distinguished European visitors. As he explained, "East Asian and Soviet opportunities will grow by themselves at Washington. My job is to provide opportunities for faculty not indigenously available." Utilizing support garnered from the Hewlett and other private foundations, as well as from funds he allocated for this purpose out of the provost's budget, he sought to institutionalize faculty exchanges with universities at Tübingen and a number of other major academic centers, especially in the Federal Republic of Germany, to build permanent reciprocal relationships. Through these exchanges he sought to redress the perceived Asian/European imbalance on the campus. In these efforts he concentrated on the humanities and social sciences. "The natural scientists have no trouble finding the funds once they know where they wish to go," he observed.

The exchange program also suits another of Beckmann's beliefs, namely that administrative support for faculty study abroad should be kept to an absolute minimum and rely instead on local people in the host countries. Beckmann evidently ran most of these exchange programs out of his office, and perhaps out of his hip pocket, in an effort to minimize the cost and red tape associated with building a separate faculty study abroad administrative structure.

A number of faculty applauded this effort. One senior faculty member at the Jackson School noted that the university was "built on oriental studies" and that what Beckmann had been doing was most helpful in exposing systematically to the faculty the roots of their Western values. Departments are permitted to recapture 50 percent of the funds when faculty go on leave without pay, and this encourages departments to have their faculty go abroad. One of the special features of the Tübingen arrangement is that the university sends Asianists and receives Europeanists. "There is no strategic thinking here except for Beckmann," one faculty member observed; as a result of his efforts "this university is better than it ought to be." "It takes a talent like Rosovsky's [referring to Henry Rosovsky, dean of the faculty of arts and sciences at Harvard University in the 1970s and early 1980s] to make those think they're leading when they are actually being led." "Beckmann is a master of cooptation, and his strategy provides him leverage in pitting competing values against each other." It struck us that Beckmann, whether or not one fully agrees with his approach, had been encouraging special opportunities for faculty study abroad to achieve broader institutional goals that would not have been reached without the subtle and farsighted intervention of a savvy chief academic officer.

Colorado School of Mines

The Colorado School of Mines is a high-quality institution offering rigorous technical training to about fifteen hundred undergraduates and eight hundred graduate students in Golden, Colorado, a small town less than an hour's drive west of Denver. Mines, as it is often called, has historically been strong in petroleum, geophysical, mining, and chemical engineering. Most of its graduates plan to practice their trade in Colorado and other sections of the western United States. However many non-American alumni of the institution are in influential engineering and management positions abroad. For example, the burgeoning activity of the Organization of Petroleum Exporting Countries (OPEC) brought large numbers of foreign students from these member countries to Mines in the 1970s and early 1980s.

Academic offerings in the humanities and social sciences are viewed as service courses, as at many other technical institutions. Given the mission and characteristics of the college, one would not normally expect to see much activity with respect to faculty study abroad. Although once true, however, this is now changing.

Graduates of Mines have discovered in recent years, if they did not know it before, the true meaning of global interdependence. Many U.S.-based corporations have sent Mines alumni to work overseas in Chile and other parts of Latin America, Germany, the Philippines, and elsewhere. They have learned, we were told, that the United States no longer leads the world in all the technologies relevant to mining engineering and that Americans have much to learn from how these activities are practiced elsewhere. Mineral processing and extractive metallurgical techniques are at a very advanced stage in Chile, for example. "We must be fully aware of what is happening internationally in our fields or we will be left behind," asserted one faculty member. "Most of what is significant is not in the journals. The U.S. is dominant in many practices but not in the development of new techniques."

Some departments, such as the Department of Metallurgy, have been "very international" for twenty-five years and have encouraged faculty to spend time "practicing" and studying abroad. But until recently this has been the exception at Mines, not the norm. What has begun to turn things around, ironically, stems from the views of alumni forcefully expressed to the college's board of trustees and senior administrators. One Mines graduate, a straight-A student, began to be given international tasks at his U.S.-based corporation after six years on the job. Although he is very strong technically, he was personally appalled to realize in a corporate meeting that he did not even know the location of the Philippines, let alone the nature of the geophysical activities taking place there. He reported to the college that something had to be done to educate current students about the world and the international marketplace. Another Mines alumnus was working in Chile at the time of the overthrow of the Allende regime. Because of the political instability, he was forced to leave the country, yet he did not even know who Allende was or the significance of the political developments that had led to his ouster! He, too, urged that Mines do a better job of training its students both about technical advances elsewhere in the world and about the political, cultural, and economic milieu in societies relevant to the interests of Mines alumni. As a result, the board of trustees has encouraged the college administration to invest more in internationalizing the curriculum and in providing opportunities for faculty and students to spend time abroad. "The marketplace has altered our attitudes about the importance of international experience," noted one senior faculty member. Given that about 14 percent of its students are international and that an increasingly larger percentage of its graduates will be working abroad, Mines has increased opportunities for faculty to go abroad. Enhancing the faculty's research capabilities and members' knowledge of practical techniques, which can in turn be imparted to their students, are the primary objectives of these trips. Funding remains an obstacle evidently: "Mines has an institutional goal to be international, but not the funds to implement it." Another institutional impediment is that department chairs are reticent to release their faculty for long periods because they need them to cover the many required courses of the engineering curricula. On the other hand, according to the faculty handbook, to be promoted to full professor a faculty member must have *international* recognition, which, in engineering fields, can often be acquired with a few well-placed experiences abroad.

Fulbright research grants are seen as increasingly attractive by college faculty. One senior faculty member, born in Turkey and educated in Germany, is an especially strong advocate of faculty experiences abroad: "We need to internationalize to eliminate the ugly American syndrome. It is wise to make investments in reciprocal faculty exchanges to strengthen interuniversity bonds. We have much to learn from non-Americans. The Soviets, French, Hungarians, and Chinese have done major work in thin films, emulsions, and superconductivity beyond what has been done in this country."

In order to provide institutional support to these perspectives, Mines established in 1988 the CSM International Institute, founded, according to university documents, "to serve as the School's designated clearinghouse for university-related activities and programs with international content. It is particularly concerned with advancing the cause of 'internationalizing' engineering education in an appropriate, timely and innovative fashion." The CSM International Institute serves as the school's overall coordinator in developing new teaching and research opportunities abroad and as chief agent in promoting outreach activities. Founded with grants from the Tinker Foundation, the U.S. Department of Education, the U.S. Information Agency, and the Pfizer and Exxon Education Foundations, the Institute has gotten off to a very fast start, establishing fifteen university linkages in Latin America and creating a new Pacific Rim Center to foster comparable connections in that dynamic part of the world. The Department of Global Systems and Cultures was also set up, its underlying premise being "that no engineering decision outside the United States is made on solely technical and scientific grounds but rather is political, social and economic in nature. The mandate of the department therefore is to create and offer courses with political, economic, cultural, historical, and public policy perspectives on the minerals and energy-rich countries of the Third World and their interaction with the development countries." One of the Institute's priorities is to facilitate faculty associate travel to other countries as "the method of choice for developing expertise that contributes directly to realizing" its objectives. When we visited Mines, there were already more than thirty faculty associates at the institute drawn from departments including metallurgical engineering, geophysics, mining engineering, petroleum engineering, and mathematics.

Faculty study abroad opportunities are still maturing at Mines. The establishment of the institute and the influence of important international alumni – for example, three generations of the family that owns and manages Brazil's largest corporation, one of Hong Kong's leading business people, members of the family that manages Peru's leading minerals technology company, and several key decision makers in OPEC – clearly indicate that the internationalization of the curriculum and faculty experiences abroad will be of increasing significance to the institution. On balance the case illustrates how changes in the marketplace and pressures from alumni can begin to alter deeply entrenched institutional values and practices and stimulate a search for effective ways to provide faculty experiences abroad.

8

Epilogue: missing the boat

Conditions facing U.S. academe

We have discussed how pressures emerged after World War II for
U.S. higher education to internationalize itself. Our institutions
responded fairly well to these challenges. The first challenge grew
out of the United States' new-found role as "leader of the free
world." If the United States was to contain communism abroad
and assist new nations to evolve with democratic governments
and free market economies, the American people had to understand both a great deal about friend and foe and much about the
world system that was being reconstructed from the ashes of
empires. This new need for international understanding manifested itself on campuses in two ways. First, demands were
made for area and international studies programs by students and
faculty who felt a passionate concern for these subjects and a
career commitment to understand them better. Second, requests
and financial support came from the federal government and
foundations and to a lesser extent from corporations to assist
through programs oriented to national intelligence, public diplomacy, public understanding, development assistance, and international business. Colleges and universities responded by establishing area studies centers, international affairs schools and
programs, internationally oriented courses in some professional
fields, and commitments (especially at land-grant universities) to
participate in development assistance programs overseas.

The net effect of the academic response to the perceived needs
for global understanding was the creation of internationally sophisticated enclaves, mainly in the social sciences and humanities

and parts of the professional schools. Their individual accomplishments were impressive, but the rest of the institutions remained relatively untouched by the world; those unaffected were sometimes hostile, but more often they were tolerant and unconcerned so long as the new structures did not threaten established interests. A term often used to describe these enclaves is *marginalized;* their tenuous status in many places was demonstrated by the fact that they were rarely considered major intellectual foci within their home disciplines, and the retirement or departure of one or two key figures was often enough to bring to an end an international program. Such developments would not have had this effect on units like the business school or the chemistry department. The multidisciplinary nature of international programs made them especially vulnerable.

We do not mean to imply for a moment that higher education made only a feeble response to the call it received. With the help of National Defense Education Act (NDEA) and private funds, academe developed distinguished language and area competence. Through the Fulbright program it made friends abroad and improved international understanding. By cooperating with AID and multilateral agencies, it advanced a foreign policy of help to the needy and worthy and gave graduates of some professional schools an international sophistication. But the point is, all of this did not internationalize the institutions broadly. Overall they remained largely unaffected. The response of higher education to this initial set of challenges presented by the United States' new world role was not unlike the early actions of the federal government, which also created specialized organs to deal with the situation (for example, the National Security Council, the Central Intelligence Agency) while leaving the rest of the federal bureaucracy (for example, the Commerce, Labor, and Treasury departments) largely untouched.

The first set of needs for internationalization was presented squarely to U.S. higher education during the 1940s, 1950s, and 1960s. The second set came in the 1970s and 1980s and was, in contrast to the first, generated by students, both foreign and domestic. In the 1970s, without very much effort on their part, U.S.

institutions became the beneficiaries of a wave of popularity around the world. Students came to the United States in droves, from countries rich and poor, north and south, supported by aid or paying their own way. Over the two decades the numbers rose from around 125,000 to more than 350,000. Foreign students came to research universities, community colleges, and everything in between. In the 1980s the relatively small stream of Americans going abroad for study also increased, for a host of reasons ranging from financial advantages to the quest for foreign language competence and a simple desire to see the world.

A distinct difference in the response to this second wave of pressures for internationalization, apart from the establishment of foreign student and study abroad offices, was that practically no significant institutional adjustments were made in response to it. The flood of foreign students lapped on the shores with hardly a notice in many places, except perhaps occasional expressions of welcome or annoyance. Curricula were seldom adjusted, and faculty felt few pressures to understand better the world from which these students came. In the heyday of the "American century" there was little felt need for the "center" to adjust to the needs of the "periphery." Study abroad for Americans has been accommodated quite well in some institutions, but once more without leading generally to any widespread institutional internationalization. Before departing, students are seldom prepared for their experience and returnees are barely acknowledged at all for their accomplishment.

By the end of the 1980s U.S. colleges and universities had faced four decades of challenge to internationalize and had partially responded, without changing fundamentally their character as domestically oriented institutions, holding the United States and not the world as their natural constituency. The innate conservatism of academe had resisted pressures for organic change.

As we enter the 1990s, U.S. higher education is facing a third challenge to internationalize, a third set of needs. If the response to this challenge is not more profound and institutionally creative than responses to the past two, we believe that the costs to the nation will be great. All involved will pay heavily this time for missing the boat. To a degree far greater than at any time in the past, the world is an integrated whole. This generalization holds at every level. The most urgent problems facing humankind cannot any longer be thought to stop at national borders: Population growth, disease, environmental degradation, arms races, terrorism – none of these can be perceived any longer as someone else's problem or as ours alone. They are ours collectively. A highly integrated world economy means that business practices, legal systems, engineering tasks, and food production can no longer be viewed exclusively from a domestic perspective. They all are global issues. Those who persevere in a parochial approach to these subjects cut themselves off from prospective solutions and impose unacceptable costs on themselves and on the world. Even the conception of national security as a purely military problem has lost much of its rationale. Fortress America is simply not a viable option. What good are so-called secure borders if nuclear fallout from some third-party conflict half a world away decimates our own population, or if tropical deforestation and worldwide air pollution lead to global warming and inundation of our coastal cities?

Of equal significance to the academic community is the fact that the world of scholarship, too, has become global in more and more fields. U.S. dominance, probably exaggerated even at the best of times, is declining relatively in the world of scholarship as it is in the global economy. The only sensible course is for all of the U.S. scholarly community to recognize at last and as quickly as possible that the world is essential to its success, that one must stretch one's eyes, ears, and mind abroad in all that it does. It is natural in a period of scholarly dominance to believe that it will go on forever, to deny the possibility of decline, but failure to accept the changing reality is the way to accelerate the inevitable decline.

The source of the demands in this third wave of pressures for internationalization, as in the first two, is largely external to U.S. academe. They come, for example, from leaders of U.S. industry who recognize that technological advances today, as well as capital and sales, come bountifully from overseas, and they come from the creativity of intellectuals in other nations who have drawn close to and in many cases surpassed the level of accomplishment of their U.S. counterparts. Moreover, non-American scholars are increasingly rejecting a collegial relationship that requires them always to speak English and adopt the cultural mores of the American. Equality of participation along all dimensions of the scholarly relationship is increasingly demanded, but this is a condition for which many U.S. scholars are unprepared.

The ticket to a smooth passage

Just as many parts of the private sector of the U.S. economy have been compelled to adapt recently to a more highly integrated world system, so U.S. higher education is called upon today to make a similar adjustment. If we act quickly, the adjustment can be made from a position of strength, rather than from the weakness that was the case for much of U.S. manufacturing industry. The trick is to wake up to impending weakness before it is too late.

The internationalization of U.S. colleges and universities that is required for the 1990s is far more profound than that accomplished in earlier decades. First of all, the existing international enclaves must be disbanded or, better still, used as the bases for new levels of internationalization throughout institutions. Comprehension of foreign languages and cultural diversity must become not simply the province of a designated few but the responsibility of all. There is every reason to be confident that U.S. scholarly research and training may remain prominent, if not necessarily preeminent, for decades to come, but it can do so only if U.S. scholars become better able to meet their competitors and potential collaborators on grounds of true equality. It is striking to see in Europe today the growth of an easy familiarity among scholars of many nations and a spirit of cooperation represented by activities like the Erasmus Program of scholarly exchanges. A similar atmosphere is growing across East Asia and in Latin America. In pursuing scholarly integration across national

borders, Americans would be simply joining a worldwide movement in which others are in the vanguard.

The precise benefits to be achieved by disciplines from greater
international involvement will vary widely and may be only dimly
perceived in some fields. Indeed, the benefits are likely to be
grasped finally in some cases only after mature reflection on their
experiences. We recorded above the sense in many parts of applied science of the urgent need for continuing and complex contacts abroad, contrasted with parts of the natural and physical
sciences, where a belief in domestic omnipotence reigns su-
preme. As our conviction grew during the course of this study
about the potential benefits from cross-cultural interactions in all
areas of scholarship, we were led naturally to reflect on our own
fields of specialization. There, in both cases, we were confirmed
in our belief about the potential benefits, some of which cannot be
identified immediately.

In order to probe the economics case, we asked a particularly
distinguished leader of the discipline about the utility to U.S.
economists of extended time abroad. His immediate reaction was
very similar to that of many physical scientists we had heard on
our travels. "There are lots of bright people abroad," he said.
"Many of them were my students, and they come back to see me
often, or I drop in on them. It is useful for us to talk. But their
best work appears in our journals, and there is no particular point
in spending a period with them at home except to have a good
time." We were startled then to hear this same economist rise in a
public meeting one day later and say, "I was asked yesterday
about the utility of time spent abroad. At the moment I was
unable to see benefits. Since then I have had further reflections.
Our graduates are indeed dominant in many countries of the
world, and we have close continuing contacts with them. But
then I thought to myself that our graduates are not dominant in
many of the most economically successful countries of the world,
for example, Japan and West Germany. I don't know exactly
what economics is being used by the economists who advise policy makers in these countries, but it isn't ours. I tried to speak

with them to find out, but I could not speak their language either figuratively or literally. Now I think perhaps we should know more about this unfamiliar economics, both so that we can understand better Japanese and German behavior and policy and because they may have depth of insight that we lack." The point in reciting this anecdote is not to imply that this distinguished economist was necessarily right in his intuition, but rather to suggest that leaders of many disciplines may discern hitherto unrecognized opportunities abroad if only they are pressed to look hard.

The other field in which we work, national security studies, has been jolted in recent years by changing world conditions perhaps as much as any other in the social sciences. From a situation in the 1960s, when security problems were perceived mainly as a product of the East-West conflict, and understandable through reference to culture-free rational actor models of strategic behavior, security has come to be seen as inextricably tied to the behavior of Afghan tribesmen, Iranian fundamentalists, Nicaraguan revolutionaries, Panamanian and Iraqi dictators, and even tropical deforestation and global warming. The new players in the security game, it becomes clear, cannot be understood through any mechanical modeling exercise. Deep cultural knowledge and sophistication are required of the analyst – qualities not yet possessed by many strategists. Strategic studies without international studies become empty. Once again, our purpose is not to criticize strategic studies, but rather to suggest that, like other parts of the scholarly community, it has discovered that it has much to gain from a true internationalization across a broad front.

Both economics and national security studies had their own "micro" versions of the early responses of the U.S. scholarly community to the first demands for internationalization. They created a few special posts for internationalists in subfields called comparative systems or foreign area studies or given some other designation. The opportunity today for them and others lies not with more of that approach, but with broad internationalization across the face of these disciplines.

The internationalization of the nineties cannot be the responsibility of a few on campus who are assigned to do those foreign tasks. It must become part of the central mission of an institution, not just a piece of presidential rhetoric or some phrases in the case for reaccreditation. It must inform and infuse the regulations of institutions and also the rules of the game. Above all, U.S. scholars in the 1990s, whether students or faculty, must be expected routinely to acquire sophisticated knowledge of the world: of foreign language, of other cultures, of other perspectives. They must learn to perceive issues globally and understand the nature of international political and economic systems. International sophistication must become as much an expected part of student and faculty performance as acquaintance with a research literature or a kit of tools. And the incentive structures and support systems of academe must be reformed to reflect these values.

Recommendations

Returning now to the main theme of this study, we conclude that scholarly experience abroad is the best route in the short run by which U.S. higher education can prepare itself to respond positively to the current challenge to internationalize. Indeed, there are few other routes open. For students and senior faculty alike, in applied areas and pure, direct human contact abroad is an immediate way to exchange ideas, arrange collaboration, and generate intellectual products. But increased scholarly experience abroad, and the campus internationalization it will generate, will not occur spontaneously. It will require enlightened action at all levels of the scholarly community. The following list gives points for urgent consideration. There is much that all those who have roles in the enterprise of U.S. higher education can do to achieve the goal of true internationalization through a well-traveled and cosmopolitan professoriate.

1. Institutions of higher education

The institutions of higher education are probably the most important actors. They have multiple tasks. The first set is introspective. Institutions must examine carefully their rules and regulations, incentive structures, statements of purpose, and other features that condition the behavior of faculty, staff, and students. Our travels through higher education persuaded us of the complexity of the constraints on faculty who pursue international experience today. Some of these constraints are there by design; others seem to be accidental. Some constraints are embedded in codes and symbols that warn faculty of the hazards to careers in extended periods away from domestic tasks. Punishments are imposed on those who ignore these codes: They incur relative downward adjustments in compensation, upward adjustments in workload, and various barriers to advancement. Sometimes a long-standing administrative tradition, such as failing to leave a faculty salary with the unit from which a faculty member departs, may be a serious impediment to travel. Failure to make provision for fringe benefits and increments to compensation during an absence surely is.

The second set of institutional tasks is to match the encouragement of international experience to its perceived value to the institution. There has been a widespread belief in many institutions that, except in a few obvious subdisciplines, the benefits of international experience are mainly personal and undeserving of institutional reward. We suggest that this position, if ever justified, is demonstrably anachronistic today. Just as institutions encourage their faculty to attend meetings and present papers, they should encourage them to gain international competence, including an understanding of language and culture. Just how vigorous this encouragement should become, and what form it should take, must depend on the circumstances and judgment of institutional leaders. But our impressions are that the real benefits are typically greater than current assessments. Institutions can encourage faculty by providing a generous sabbatical system, with some coverage of travel costs; by offering to provide part of the travel costs if the remainder can be raised externally (topping up or paying fringe benefits associated with specific awards to visit foreign countries, such as Fulbrights); by giving demonstrable recognition of successful internationalization through salary increments; by negotiating exchange arrangements with foreign institutions; and by supporting innovative devices to get faculty overseas, including a "research tail" attached to study abroad directorships. Public expression of institutional commitment to internationalization is also crucial, but it is of limited value if not backed up by resources.

2. Faculty members

Internationalists among the faculty should band together to promote institutional change. But outside the enclaves they have proved to be especially vulnerable. We suggest that devices are needed for mutual support and protection. These might be organized around traditional international studies units; however, enclave dwellers themselves are sometimes among the most hostile to institution-wide internationalization. Perhaps lessons can be drawn from women and minority faculty, who in recent years have developed networks and other support mechanisms. We found on our travels that on some campuses former Fulbrighters and others who were experiencing discrimination and other costs because of their international interests had not met each other across departments before our visit. Banded together in some way, perhaps under the umbrella of faculty government, they would be able better to make the case for the value of their experience.

3. Professional associations and accrediting agencies

Professional associations and accrediting agencies of various kinds should impel change in institutional mores. These bodies are typically better attuned to the needs and realities of the outside world and are unaffected by the conservatism of campus special interests. The role of the AACSB in impelling the internationalization of the field of business administration is remarkable. Similar bodies in other professional areas should consider taking comparable steps. Regional accrediting bodies for entire colleges and universities could also make a major contribution to higher

education and the nation at large by imposing on institutions a
degree of serious self-study of this question that they would not
be prepared to undertake on their own.

4. Agencies of government

The agencies of government at the federal, state, and municipal
levels should recognize the critical importance to their jurisdic-
tions of the thorough internationalization of higher education.
Moreover, they should recognize that in most cases the assistance mechanisms they have in place were devised for an earlier
era and are aimed mainly either at assistance to the enclaves of
internationalists on campus or at brief conference excursions
abroad. Indeed, some government units still retain anachronistic
regulations, such as a prohibition on, or special approval required
for, foreign travel and overseas telephone calls.

It is, of course, necessary that those in government continue to
support the enclaves to the extent that they value the services
provided, for example, intelligence about foreign areas, citizen
understanding of international affairs, and participation in development assistance and public diplomacy. But the larger and
broader values of internationalization must now be appreciated as
well. And this extended appreciation should dictate the interest of
government departments well beyond the usual sources of interest in the State Department, AID, USIA, the Department of Education, and NSF. Internationalization of the scholarly community
and the implication it holds for the solution of national problems
and for maintaining national competitiveness dictate the participation of the Commerce, Labor, Agriculture, Energy, and
Transportation departments, as well as the Treasury. Clearly,
with such widespread significance now attached to internationalization and such haphazard support for it from existing programs,
this is an appropriate time for the formulation of a new, comprehensive national policy.

The continental vastness of the United States and the relative
homogeneity of its population have been important factors con-
tributing to the growth and stability of the nation. The United

States has had for two centuries what Europe is striving to achieve and Latin America sees as only a flicker of hope. But our size and character have also raised barriers to a wider global integration, and it is highly appropriate for the federal government in particular to assume leadership in combating these costs.

5. Private and corporate foundations

A traditional function for both private and corporate foundations is stimulation of and support for innovation. They should aid innovative programs of internationalization. Today, innovative and experimental programs to achieve internationalization are urgently demanded and present a new set of opportunities for philanthropy. We remain largely locked into modes of exchange and cooperation that were devised decades ago. Many forms of new linkages abroad among all kinds of educational and research institutions, individual scholars and students, and private agencies should be explored, tested, and adopted if found worthy. Relationships may or may not flourish among institutes, departments, and professional societies if properly nourished, but the only way to find out is to try, and short-term funding will make this possible.

The internationalization of the U.S. campus, and the means to this end, the stimulation of international sophistication among the faculty, are subjects that should hold the attention of policy makers at many levels in the years ahead. This study only scratches the surface of the issues involved. It will be reward enough to us if these observations and reflections stimulate the discussion and debates that are the prelude to action.

Appendix: institutions visited

I. Colorado
1. Colorado College, Colorado Springs
2. Colorado School of Mines, Golden
3. Colorado State University, Fort Collins
4. United States Air Force Academy, Colorado Springs
5. University of Colorado, Boulder
6. University of Denver, Denver

II. Georgia
1. Atlanta University, Atlanta
2. Emory University, Atlanta
3. Georgia Institute of Technology, Atlanta
4. Georgia State University, Atlanta
5. Spellman College, Atlanta
6. University of Georgia, Athens

III. Massachusetts
1. Amherst College, Amherst
2. Babson College, Waltham
3. Bunker Hill Community College, Boston
4. Hampshire College, Amherst
5. Harvard University, Cambridge
6. Massachusetts Institute of Technology, Cambridge
7. Northeastern University, Boston
8. Simmons College, Boston
9. University of Massachusetts at Boston, Boston
10. Wheaton College, Norton

IV. Oregon
1. Lewis and Clark College, Portland
2. Oregon State University, Corvallis
3. Reed College, Portland
4. University of Oregon, Eugene

V. South Carolina
1. University of South Carolina, Columbia

VI. Utah
1. Brigham Young University, Provo
2. University of Utah, Salt Lake City
3. Utah State University, Logan
4. Weber State College, Ogden

VII. Washington
1. Evergreen State College, Olympia
2. Pacific Lutheran University, Takoma
3. Seattle University, Seattle
4. University of Puget Sound, Takoma
5. University of Washington, Seattle
6. Western Washington State University, Bellingham

Index